W9-AVE-666

FLORIDA STATE
UNIVERSITY LIBRARIES

SEP 20 1995

TALLAHASSEE, FLORIDA

Central African Republic

WORLD BIBLIOGRAPHICAL SERIES

General Editors:
Robert G. Neville (Executive Editor)
John J. Horton

Robert A. Myers   Ian Wallace
Hans H. Wellisch   Ralph Lee Woodward, Jr.

John J. Horton is Deputy Librarian of the University of Bradford and currently Chairman of its Academic Board of Studies in Social Sciences. He has maintained a longstanding interest in the discipline of area studies and its associated bibliographical problems, with special reference to European Studies. In particular he has published in the field of Icelandic and of Yugoslav studies, including the two relevant volumes in the World Bibliographical Series.

Robert A. Myers is Associate Professor of Anthropology in the Division of Social Sciences and Director of Study Abroad Programs at Alfred University, Alfred, New York. He has studied post-colonial island nations of the Caribbean and has spent two years in Nigeria on a Fulbright Lectureship. His interests include international public health, historical anthropology and developing societies. In addition to *Amerindians of the Lesser Antilles: a bibliography* (1981), *A Resource Guide to Dominica, 1493-1986* (1987) and numerous articles, he has compiled the World Bibliographical Series volumes on *Dominica* (1987), *Nigeria* (1989) and *Ghana* (1991).

Ian Wallace is Professor of German at the University of Bath. A graduate of Oxford in French and German, he also studied in Tübingen, Heidelberg and Lausanne before taking teaching posts at universities in the USA, Scotland and England. He specializes in contemporary German affairs, especially literature and culture, on which he has published numerous articles and books. In 1979 he founded the journal *GDR Monitor*, which he continues to edit under its new title *German Monitor*.

Hans H. Wellisch is Professor emeritus at the College of Library and Information Services, University of Maryland. He was President of the American Society of Indexers and was a member of the International Federation for Documentation. He is the author of numerous articles and several books on indexing and abstracting, and has published *The Conversion of Scripts, Indexing and Abstracting: an International Bibliography* and *Indexing from A to Z*. He also contributes frequently to *Journal of the American Society for Information Science*, *The Indexer* and other professional journals.

Ralph Lee Woodward, Jr. is Director of Graduate Studies at Tulane University, New Orleans, where he has been Professor of History since 1970. He is the author of *Central America, a Nation Divided*, 2nd ed. (1985), as well as several monographs and more than sixty scholarly articles on modern Latin America. He has also compiled volumes in the World Bibliographical Series on *Belize* (1980), *Nicaragua* (1983), and *El Salvador* (1988). Dr. Woodward edited the Central American section of the *Research Guide to Central America and the Caribbean* (1985) and is currently editor of the Central American history section of the *Handbook of Latin American Studies*.

VOLUME 152

Central African Republic

Pierre Kalck

Compiler

CLIO PRESS

OXFORD, ENGLAND · SANTA BARBARA, CALIFORNIA
DENVER, COLORADO

© Copyright 1993 by Clio Press Ltd.

All rights reserved. No part of this publication may be reproduced, stored in any retrieval system, or transmitted in any form or by any means, electronic, mechanical, photocopying or otherwise, without the prior permission in writing of the publishers.

British Library Cataloguing in Publication Data

Central African Republic. – (World bibliographical series; vol. 152)
I. Kalck, Pierre   II. Series
016.96741

ISBN 1–85109–172–6

Clio Press Ltd.,
55 St. Thomas' Street,
Oxford OX1 1JG, England.

ABC-CLIO,
130 Cremona Drive,
Santa Barbara,
CA 93116, USA.

Designed by Bernard Crossland.
Typeset by Columns Design and Production Services Ltd, Reading, England.
Printed and bound in Great Britain by
Bookcraft (Bath) Ltd., Midsomer Norton

THE WORLD BIBLIOGRAPHICAL SERIES

This series, which is principally designed for the English speaker, will eventually cover every country (and many of the world's principal regions), each in a separate volume comprising annotated entries on works dealing with its history, geography, economy and politics; and with its people, their culture, customs, religion and social organization. Attention will also be paid to current living conditions – housing, education, newspapers, clothing, etc.– that are all too often ignored in standard bibliographies; and to those particular aspects relevant to individual countries. Each volume seeks to achieve, by use of careful selectivity and critical assessment of the literature, an expression of the country and an appreciation of its nature and national aspirations, to guide the reader towards an understanding of its importance. The keynote of the series is to provide, in a uniform format, an interpretation of each country that will express its culture, its place in the world, and the qualities and background that make it unique. The views expressed in individual volumes, however, are not necessarily those of the publisher.

VOLUMES IN THE SERIES

Contents

Contents

Preface

The volumes in the *World Bibliographical Series* are essentially intended for English-speaking readers and consequently previous compilers have given priority to works published in the English language. The present work, however, which is devoted to the Central African Republic, forms a notable exception to this rule. This country is one of the least-known African nations and relevant works in English are few in number. At the outset, I would therefore like to explain why most of the work which has been published on the Central African Republic is written in French. In addition, I would like to investigate the development of the literature concerning the Central African Republic and describe my own involvement in Central African Republic studies.

It is a truism that, at the end of the last century, it was English-speaking men who were amongst the first Westerners to explore this 'terra incognita'. The English officer and governor of Bahr al-Ghazal, Frank Lupton, was in 1883 the first European to reach the Kotto River. Moreover, the Scottish pastor, George Grenfell, and the American, Sims, journeyed up the Ubangi in 1884 preceding the Belgians and the French. Notwithstanding this, in the following hundred years, the exploration and study of the country was carried out exclusively by French-speakers: French or Belgian explorers; then French administrators, officers and missionaries. Very few copies of their books or reports, written in the French language, were printed. Those that were printed were subjected to a very restricted distribution. None were translated into English. Published in Paris (or even Brussels) they remained almost unknown, not only in the colony itself, but throughout the rest of the world. This domination of the French language was reflected in the country's education system where French was also the language of instruction. The French established about ten state and private elementary schools in the colony but the education system developed with disconcerting slowness. Indeed the first secondary school was not created in Bangui until 1953.

For years the only reference books that one could consult, in the few rare specialised libraries in Paris, remained the works by the French colonial administrators Georges Bruel (1918 then 1931) and Felix Eboué (1933). In 1959, my book *Réalités Obanguiennes*, kindly prefaced by President Barthélemy Boganda a few weeks before his death, was received as the only existing comprehensive work on Ubangi-Shari, which became independent on 1 December 1958 and took the name of the Central African Republic. In 1960, French was proclaimed to be the official language of the new state. Sango, the country's lingua franca, was established as the national language.

During the thirty years that followed, despite the political upheavals, France continued to send to the Central African Republic, each year, more than 400 highly qualified teachers, researchers and technicians. Some of them undertook remarkable work on the country, notably in the fields of geography, geology, botany, ethnography, sociology, history and archaeology. In-depth studies were carried out with a view to developing the country's infrastructure, agriculture, animal breeding, forestry and the mining industry. Various French research institutes assured the publication of an appreciable number of these works but none were translated into English.

In 1970, at the Sorbonne, under the supervision of Hubert Deschamps, I attended a viva for a Higher Doctoral Thesis in Arts (Central African history from the earliest times to ca. 1970), in order to establish a programme to investigate the near and distant past of Central Africa. The following year Colin Legum, an English journalist specialising in African affairs (assisted by my friend Philippe Decraene) invited me to write a general work to be translated into English entitled *Central African Republic: a failure in decolonization* for his Pall Mall Library of African Affairs. At this time we were all conscious of an important anomaly i.e., the Central Africa Republic had been admitted as a member of the United Nations and yet the country had been almost totally neglected by scholars. Later, in 1980, in the same spirit, Jan Woronoff asked me to write a volume devoted to the Central African Republic for a series of historical dictionaries published by Scarecrow Press of Metuchen, New Jersey; a second edition of this book was published in May 1992. Both editions of my historical dictionary were translated into English by Professor Thomas O'Toole (currently director of African Studies at St. Cloud State University) who lived in the Central African Republic after being sent by the American government to teach at the new Faculty of Arts and Human Sciences in Bangui. The two books referred to above have at least allowed the Central African Republic to become better known amongst English and North American Africanists.

Nevertheless, books written in English about this country still remain few and far between. Of those that have appeared, three deserve a special mention. My translator and friend, Thomas O'Toole, published a book entitled *The Central African Republic: the Continent's Hidden Heart* (Boulder, Colorado: Westview; London: Gower, 1986) which provides a good overall consideration of the country. Professor Dennis D. Cordell (Madison, University of Wisconsin) published *Dar-Al-Kuti and the Last years of the trans-Saharan Slave trade* (Madison, Wisconsin: University of Wisconsin Press, 1984). Cordell spent some time in the northeast of the Central African Republic and his study includes a comprehensive history of Dar al-Kuti (1830–1911) which was the only Muslim state to be established in Central African territory. Finally, the Canadian pastor, William J. Samarin, from Toronto, is the author of a remarkable series of works in the English-language concerning the Central African languages and ethnography. Research for these books was carried out by Samarin when he was working in Ubangi-Shari as a missionary.

In addition to the authors referred to above, I should also indicate that several important, but more technical, articles written in English have been published in the United States about specialised subjects including: the Pygmies; and a vast magnetic anomaly (the existence of which was first revealed by satellite), the maximum intensity of which can be found in the Central African Republic.

In view of the fact that so few studies in English of the Central African Republic have appeared, I had to consider whether, or not, it was appropriate to include in the bibliography references to the Central African Republic gleaned from general reference works and yearbooks. Unfortunately, as with similar books written in French, these general reference books contain regrettable mistakes. Some of these errors are the result of false, mistaken or tendentious dispatches from the press agencies. In particular, I would like to mention the dispatches written in 1983 at the instigation of Bangui's military junta, which described a movement which never existed (the Central African Revolutionary Party) and a provisional government for national salvation (in exile) that was never formed. These dispatches had been fabricated in order to enable the general-president Kolingba to justify the multiple and arbitrary arrests and imprisonments that he carried out. Unfortunately, this example is not unique in a country where freedom of expression and information has been non-existent. Accordingly, I have severely limited references of this type and have endeavoured to include only those publications based on reliable sources. In the field of economics, for example, I have directed the reader to the quarterly and annual publications in English of The Economic Intelligence Unit (The Economist, London) and to the periodicals and yearbooks, in French, edited by Ediafric et Marchés Tropicaux.

In line with the general policy of the *World Bibliographical Series*, I have avoided citing articles appearing in the popular English and French press concerning such ludicrous events as the crowning of the madman-emperor, and tragic events such as the massacre of children perpetrated by the same psychopath. This type of newspaper article emanating often from the tabloid, some would say the 'gutter', press tends to present an exaggerated and simplistic view of the Central African Republic. I have therefore concentrated on more serious studies which help to provide an explanation of why such events as those referred to above occurred.

Many volumes in this Series contain chapters on 'The Press' and 'Archives' but it was not possible to include such chapters in the present volume. There are still no national archives in the Central African Republic. All that exists is a limited number of repositories containing some documents saved from destruction by David Dacko, and entrusted by him to either the National School of Administration and Magistrature, or the Boganda Museum in Bangui. The main archival source for the country remains the Overseas Section of the French National Archives, situated in Aix-en-Provence, which is completely open to the public. There is no local press in the Central African Republic, except for a small duplicated daily bulletin, with a small circulation and distribution (*Elé Songo*). Occasionally there are also propaganda magazines devoted entirely to praising the Head of State and the government. To my knowledge, there is no archive collection of these publications of any importance. Moreover, it must be pointed out that revues devoted to the African continent published in Europe and America contain few articles, or reports, concerning the Central African Republic.

Acknowledgements

I would like to thank all my French, American, English and Central African friends who have given me such valuable assistance in compiling this bibliography.

Special thanks go to: Reverend Father Ghislain de Banville, an historian of the Central African church, who systematically made an inventory of all the publications concerning the Central African Republic; to Jean Cantournet, former director of a cotton company, who methodically assessed the numerous geographical and administrative archives, which until then had remained unknown to the public; to Professor Eric de Dampierre, the distinguished expert on the peoples of east Central Africa, who is in charge of an excellent collection at the University of Paris X, entitled 'Recherches Oubanguiennes'; and above all to my friend, Yves Boulvert, head of research at ORSTOM, who during a stay of more than twenty years in the Central African Republic drew a series of excellent maps which I have found most valuable.

I would also like to thank several researchers from the French Cooperative Aid, whom I met at several symposia organised by the Institute of the History of Overseas Countries (IHPOM) at the University of Provence, and who kept me regularly informed about their research and discoveries (notably, Pierre Mollion, Jean-Dominique Pénel, Pierre Soumille and Pierre Vidal). The different French Overseas Research Institutes and the various cooperative aid organizations have, in addition, generously sent me lists of reports and studies, established in their respective fields of interest. My friend, Thomas O'Toole, has kept me informed about the limited number of new publications written in English, concerning the Central African Republic.

Amongst the Central Africans who have courteously replied to my requests for information, I must particularly thank President Abel Goumba, a professor of medicine and first head of government, who has been my friend for thirty-five years; the former ministers, Bernard-Christian Ayandho and Jean-Louis Psimhis, with whom I have worked over the years in various international conferences; and the Vice-Chancellor of the University of Bangui who sent me details of all the studies carried out by students at his university.

I am also grateful to my faithful translator, Lindell Aspinall, who spared no time or effort, and to Dr. Robert Neville, of Clio Press, and his wife, Georgina L. Neville, for their detailed editorial and translation work. Finally, I would like to thank my daughter, Catherine, who helped me to prepare the final manuscript.

Paris, October 1992

Introduction

On 1 December 1958, the French overseas territory of Ubangi-Shari became a member state of the French Community, under the name of the Central African Republic. On 13 August 1960, it gained independence and on 20 September in the same year, was admitted to the United Nations.

The term 'Central African Republic' was chosen in 1958 by Barthélemy Boganda, deputy for Ubangi-Shari and president of the 'Grand Conseil de l'Afrique Equatoriale Française', to apply to the whole of French Equatorial Africa. The Ubangian leader, in fact, hoped to see the four territories – which had formed French Equatorial Africa since 1910 (Chad, Ubangi-Shari, Moyen-Congo and Gabon) – attain independence as a group. He dreamed of transforming the old colonial federation into a unified state, which would form the nucleus of an even larger union, the United States of Latin Africa, bringing together the various possessions of France, Belgium, Portugal and Spain in Central Africa. This dream was not realized, and the Central African Republic was to include only the territory of Ubangi-Shari.

Ravaged by the hunt for slaves, the territory of Central Africa that exists today, constituted the last blank on the maps of Africa. Pillaged, even before being exploited, it thus acquired the nickname the 'Cinderella of the French Empire'. The most land-locked country of the African continent, the Central African Republic is listed amongst the most impoverished countries of the international community. Although it possesses real possibilities for development, its main handicap is that it is not well-known to all those who could play a part in its destiny.

This work aims at improving our knowledge of the Central African Republic. It offers the reader bibliographical references, each specially selected and with accompanying comments, arranged under several different chapter headings. The introduction briefly explains the main characteristics of the Central African Republic and is divided into the following sections: the country; its inhabitants; its history, its institutions; and its economy.

The country

The Central African Republic, in the shape of a vast trapezium, is located in the very heart of the continent and covers an area of 618,135 square kilometres (greater than that of France and the Benelux countries put together).

The present-day borders of the Central African Republic are those of the former territory of Ubangi-Shari in 1958. They are the result of either agreements made long ago between colonial powers, or administrative measures taken by the former authorities. The border with Zaïre (the course of the Mbomu, and then the Ubangi rivers), was fixed by agreements between France and King Leopold II (1887-94). The one with Sudan results from the Franco-British agreement of 1899, and the border with Cameroon from the Franco-German agreements (1894-1908), re-established by the Treaty of Versailles at the end of the First World War. The borders between the Central African Republic and the republics of Chad and Congo, are the limits fixed long ago by the former territories of French Equatorial Africa, finally modified in 1936.

These international borders are sometimes qualified arbitrarily. Although they divide into several Central African ethnic groups, they correspond to a region presenting a certain physical unity: the Ubangian sill. Separating the Chad and the Congo Basins, it stretches, from west to east, from the basin of the Niger (Benue River) to the basin of the Nile (Bahr al-Ghazal).

Geographical and geological surveys of this comparatively recently explored country, were, for a long time, few in number. Aerial photography, satellite pictures, and in particular studies carried out on the ground during a period of twenty-five years, by French technicians have, however, led to more precise mapping of the country. Recent works have also allowed a better perception of the landscape, geology, hydrography, climate and vegetation of the Central African Republic.

The Central African ridge between the Ubangi and the Shari rivers is made up of a Precambrian platform. From an average altitude of 500 metres, it rises progressively towards the east (the Dar Chala massif reaching a height of 1330 metres), and more sharply towards the west (the Yadé massif reaching a height of 1410 metres). This platform sinks in the north into a region called the Chad depression made up of recent alluvial deposits (quaternary). In the east (Nzako), in the northeast (Birao), and in the southwest (Bambio), we find some older sandy-clay formations (tertiary). In the west and the east, the Central African territory is covered with two vast deposits of Cretaceous sandstone (secondary): the sandstone plateaux of Carnot and Mouka-Ouadda.

Since the discovery of the country, the complexity and density of the network of waterways has been the subject of special studies. One-third of this network belongs to the Chad basin and two-thirds to that of the Congo. The Logone and the Shari rivers, which have their sources in Central Africa under the names of the Pendé and the Ouham, feed Lake Chad, which is what remains of a vast inland sea and which forms the centre of the largest endoreic basin in the world after Australia. The Ubangi river, which is the main tributary of the Congo and measures the same length as the Danube, deserves like the Sangha, the albeit erroneous title of *fleuve*. These two large rivers have been, and remain, the principal routes of penetration into Central Africa. The rivers and streams which make up the Central African basins of Pendé-Logone, Ouham-Shari, Ubangi and Sangha, are numerous, abundant and sometimes of an impressive length (Kotto, Chinko, Lobaye). The course that these waterways follow is governed by tectonics and waterfalls or rapids appear where low rocks become escarpments.

Like the rest of the continent situated between the Equator and the Tropic of Cancer, the climate of Central Africa is influenced by two air masses: tropical boreal and tropical austral. The flux resulting from the oscillation of the Libyan anticyclone in the north and the anticyclone of Sainte Hélène in the south, divides the year into two seasons: the rainy season (between June and September, the most extensive period of Atlantic high pressure); and the dry season (between October and May, the period during which there is a weak development of the Libyan anticyclone). The climate is more humid in the south, and becomes progressively drier in the north (e.g. there is a rainy season of 304 days in Salo, on the Sangha in the extreme south, and of 132 days in Birao, in the extreme northeast). The annual rainfall is as high as 1,806 millimetres at Rafaï in the Mbomu Valley, and drops to 843 millimetres at Birao. The average annual temperatures range between 23.4° (Bouar), and 26.5° (Birao). The annual hours of sunshine are about 2,100 hours at Bangui.

Reflecting these climatic divisions, a zone occupied by a dense evergreen forest (the northern part of the Great Equatorial Forest), running from south to north, gives way to a forested savanna, the remnants of dense, dry, primitive forests, followed by a zone resembling the steppes. The study of the soils in these various zones has been intensified in recent years. Three-quarters of the country is covered in ferralytic soils. The warm and abundant rainfall leads to deep hydrolysis of the rock minerals. It is estimated that a quarter of the territory of Central Africa could easily be cultivated, although present-day cultivation represents barely one per cent of the area of the country. The east, which is currently unpopulated, contains a wealth of untapped resources and forms an edaphic reserve on a continental scale.

Central Africa's low population has resulted in the preservation of an exceptionally rich variety of wildlife. The Central African Republic has at its disposal three national parks and eight game reserves, the supervision of which is difficult. Unfortunately, poaching and ivory-trading are threatening to destroy the efforts which have been made to conserve this heritage.

The people

There are many obstacles to obtaining reliable information concerning population statistics in the Central African Republic. This is due to: the near-absence of a civil service; the persistence of a head tax created by the colonial authorities at the turn of the century which dissuades individuals from presenting themselves to the census organizers; and a fear amongst some ethnic groups of revealing themselves as a greater burden on the state than other ethnic groups.

The population surveys carried out in 1960, 1965, 1975 and 1989, (this last one unpublished), give the following figures: 1,203,000; 1,440,000; 1,822,379; and 2,611,000. Since the 1965 census underestimated the total, the Central African government decreed that the country's population rose to 2,088,000 inhabitants in 1966. In 1974, an official document increased the estimated population figure to 3,000,000 inhabitants, 300,000 of which live in Bangui.

The annual population growth in Central Africa is estimated at 2.5%. This rate results from the difference between a birth rate of approximately 4.5% and a death rate of around 2%. Although the birth rate in the country is in general high, except in the east, there is an extremely high death rate among children. More than one-fifth of all children do not reach the age of five. It is estimated that today children under fifteen years of age constitute forty per cent of the population of Central Africa. Life expectancy, however, is no more than forty-five years of age. More than ten per cent of the population in the town of Bangui is thought to be HIV positive. It should also be noted that the population projections, like those provided by United Nations annual statistics, do not take into account the problems of providing accurate information. It is probable that the projected figure of 3,000,000 inhabitants, will not be reached until the end of this century at the earliest. The estimate of 2,741,550 inhabitants could be held back for 1991, the real figure being probably less. The population of the Central African Republic can be described as miniscule in relation to the size of the territory, even if the official over-estimates are used. Moreover, the population is spread throughout the country in a manner that is far from homogeneous. The four prefectures in the east of Central Africa account for only six per cent of the population in an area which covers more than forty per cent of the country.

The town of Bangui is expanding continually because of the high rural exodus. The population, which reached about 90,000 inhabitants 30 years ago, was estimated at 450,000 inhabitants in 1989. By now it could have reached half a million inhabitants, a fifth of the population of the whole country. In addition, it is divided into one hundred districts, within which the inhabitants are forced to pursue agricultural activities as their only means of subsistence.

Outside the capital, the official classification of population is divided between the so-called rural zones and urban centres. This distribution, inherited from the colonial period, is somewhat arbitrary. All the towns, however small, are in fact noted urban centres that have developed around former colonial administrative posts and have become county towns of prefectures, or sub-prefectures, or even simple administrative control posts. Seven of these urban centres, with a combined population of between 20,000 and 40,000 inhabitants, (in order of importance: Bambari, Berbérati, Bouar, Bossangoa, Carnot, Bangassou and Kaga-Bandoro), can be classifed as towns. The 'town' of Bimbo, which has grown up around a former administrative post near Bangui, is growing at the same pace as the capital, of which it is today a suburb.

In the actual rural zones themselves, there are some 7,000 populated areas, called villages, which have been established along the roads and tracks used by cars, and the banks of the Ubangi. They are grouped into cantons, or rural districts.

During the colonial period, the authorities emphasized that the ethnic groups settling in Ubangi-Shari should be diverse. Accordingly, on this territory one could meet the tallest men in the world (Sara), and also the smallest (Pygmies). It is true that at a glance the Central African population seems to divide itself into a high number of ethnic and sub-ethnic groups, often overlapping each other. In the course of their little-known history, they have been subjected to a multitude of transformations: they have merged with the old occupants, they have formed new ethnic groups, they have divided or migrated and, sometimes even disappeared. Some people prefer to group the Central Africans according to the natural environment governing their way of life: the inhabitants of the great forest; the populations of the savanna; and those who live on the banks of the Ubangi. In reality, the Central African population is made up of a limited number of ethnic groups, more easily identified by the vernacular language that they speak than by their physical characteristics, and all of them connected by the same cultural traits.

The Banda and the Gbaya make up the largest number of inhabitants in the Central African Republic. The greatest part of the inhabited savanna is their territory, although some of them are found in isolated groups in the heart of the dense Central African forest, or beyond the national borders (Cameroon, Zaïre, Bahr al-Ghazal). Several other ethnic groups can be traced back to the Gbaya, who speak a similar language, such as the Manja who are settled in the centre of the country. The Banda, the Gbaya and the Manja at present form the majority ethnic groups in the town of Bangui.

In the north of the Central African Republic live a substantial number of the 'tall people', the Sara. Until 1936, this people that today makes up the majority group in the neighbouring republic of Chad, lived almost entirely in the territory of Ubangi-Shari. In the northwest some of the Mbum people can be found. They have mainly settled in Cameroon, on the high lands of the Adamawa massif. Mention should also be made of some formerly powerful people, who long ago moved over the vast territory of the Central African savanna, but who nowadays make up some residual groups, notably the Sabanga and the Kreich.

In the southeast of Central Africa, as well as in Zaïre and in Sudan, several warrior clans, the Bandia or Zande, succeeded in the last century, in subjugating both the Nzakara people (who were descended from the Sabanga) and many of the Sudanese peoples, and even the Bantu. By imposing their language and their institutions upon them, they created highly organized kingdoms. These Bandia and Zande states were destroyed by the European colonialists and the members of these former nations, no matter to which ethnic group they previously belonged, are now considered as an ethnic group called the Zande.

Special mention should also be made of the riverside populations of the Ubangi: the Mondjombo and Ngbaka in the great forest downstream from Bangui and the so-called Ubangian populations upstream: the Banziri and the Bouraka, the Sango, the Yakoma, the Dendi and the Bangou. The last five belong to the Ngbandi group, which is numerous in Zaïre. These diverse populations have settled on the banks of the Ubangi, in areas demarcated by rapids. Of modest size, these ethnic groups have played an important role in the history of Central Africa. They were wise traders and skilled boatmen and with the arrival of colonization, they were in constant contact with the different inland populations. The language of the Sango ethnic group formed the basis of commercial Sango (known as the water-language), which became the lingua franca of colonial Ubangi-Shari. In 1962 it was this language which was declared the national language of the Central African Republic. The Ngbaka, the Banziri, the Sango and the Yakoma provided the colonizers with their first police, militia and most of the the territory's civil servants. These ethnic groups are still dominant in the civil service and the Central African army. They have given the country its successive presidents and the majority of its politicians.

The southwest of the country is covered in dense forest and has provided a favourable refuge since time immemorial. The Aka pygmies, probably the world's oldest population, can be found there and they attract the attention of numerous scientists. Several ethnic groups, speaking Bantu, and similar to other groups settled in Zaïre and Congo, have settled in this forested region: notably the Issongo, the Pandé, the Ngoundi and the Mbimou. Their relationship with the pygmies, (whom they call the Babinga), and who have remained exclusively hunters-gatherers, is one of symbiosis.

Amongst the populations of Central Africa, the 50,000 Fulbé cattle-breeders (the Mbororo) are often overlooked, as it is common to speak only of the number of livestock they own. The Mbororo originated from Cameroon and settled with their herds on pastures in the west, the centre, and the south of Central Africa.

Foreigners from the Near East or other countries of black Africa, mainly Muslim, are engaged in many types of business operations. The number of European ex-patriates, mainly French, is small. They are found in administrative positions and large companies (numbering about 3,500). Some 1,500 French soliders have been added to this number since 1979, and are subject to frequent changes of guard (they are based at Bangui and at Bouar).

History

Thirty years ago, some people wrote that the Central African Republic represented an 'anhistoric' region. Such a judgement must now be revised. In fact it has been proved that the Central African area has been populated without a break since the appearance of man on earth. Indeed, several expeditions organized by the Natural History Museum of Paris (Roger de Bayle des Hermens 1966-68) have unearthed a wealth of prehistoric tools in the territory which now constitutes the Central African Republic. The discoveries cover the whole of prehistory, from the early Paleolithic to the Neolithic period. At approximately the same time, about one hundred megaliths (called a 'tazunu' by the Gbaya) erected near the sources of the Lobaye in the region of Bouar were investigated. At the foot of these monuments, and constructed at totally different times, the remains of an ancient agricultural civilization were brought to light.

These studies initiated further archaeological research in the Central African Republic and we now know that the appearance of iron in Central Africa can be designated to a time possibly earlier than 200-300 BC. The presence of haematite, which can be found all over Central Africa, in all probability expanded research into metallurgy. The ore could have come from Nok in the west, or Méroë in the east, these famous sites being only a few hundred kilometres away from the Central African border.

Moreover, the fact that almost ninety per cent of present-day Central Africans belong to the same linguistic group, Adamawa-Ubangian, (the sub-family Niger-Congo of the Congo-Kordofanian family, according to Greenberg's classification), proves the existence of an ancient cultural alliance, despite the many migrations, between the populations settled in this area between Cameroon and Sudan. These populations have been subjected to the greatest changes in fortune. For several centuries the fate of many Central Africans was to be bought, or captured, and then deported to distant lands. Thus Central African history, has, for at least the last four centuries, been inseparable from that of the oriental and western slave trade, Central Africa constituting a zone supplying men for both of these markets.

The River Congo and its tributaries, the Sangha and the Ubangi, were the main routes of transport for the slaves. The captives were taken from tribe to tribe and ended up at a slave gathering centre on the banks of the Stanley Pool, an expansion of the Congo River spreading between the present-day towns of Brazzaville and Kinshasa. From this pool (at that time called Poumbou, from where the brokers of the slave trade get their name of Pombeiros) the inland slaves were taken to the 'barracons' (slave parks) on the Atlantic coast. For at least three centuries these slaves, known as 'Congo', were bought from the coastal chiefs, by European slave-traders, to be transported to, and sold in, America.

The northern regions of Central Africa were the settings for real slave hunts (*ghazuas*), organized by the commercial states of Tekrour (converted country), established in the Chad Basin (Kanem-Bornu) and Gaoga, and then in Bagirmi, Ouadaï and Darfur. To the south of Aouk, Omar Djougoultoum was forced in 1826 to flee Baguirmi by his brother, Abd-el-Kader, the new Sultan. Djougoultoum fled to Wadai and the *kalak* of Wadai sent him to the Rounga in the military border area founded between the Azoum and the Aouk. In 1830 Djougoultoum created an even more southerly border area called Belad-al-Kouti as a slaving region south of the Aouk.

To the north of the Mbomou, the Bandia and Zandé kings subjugated numerous peoples in the 19th century. They welcomed the master-traders of the Upper Nile who were searching for slaves. These traders established multiple *zeribas* (fortified trading stations), and *dems* (main depots), on both sides of the Congo-Nile interfluve, which formed the departure points for numerous slave caravans. Ziber (Zobeïr or Zubayr) privileged ally of the Zandé kings, and son-in-law of Tikima the most powerful of them, from 1858 onwards took possession of the vast territories of the Kreich peoples. He became a strong ruler protected by a large army and installed in his capital Dem Zubayr in Bahr al-Ghazal he named himself Sheik. In 1874, he even conquered Darfur for Egypt. Ziber and his lieutenants then undertook numerous slave wars in Upper Ubangui, depopulating the country. Arriving in Cairo in August 1875, he was arrested by the Khedive. After Ziber's imprisonment in Cairo, his first lieutenant, Rabah, refused to serve his son. Rabah made eastern central Africa, where he recruited soldiers and slaves, a departure base for the conquest of a huge territory. Refusing to join the supporters of the Mahdi, the masters of the Sudan, he replaced the sultan of Belad-al-Kouti with his loyal supporter Muhammad as-Sanusi, and devastated Bagirmi, taking possession of Bornu. The king of Wadaï defeated Muhammad as-Sanusi, just as the French, arriving from the Ubangi, were about to completely alter the course of history in this region (1894).

During this same period, the slave trade supporters in Zanzibar, Leopold's agents, were also making inroads into the Uele-Ubangi basin. In the northwest, the lamido Fulbé of Ngaoundéré, the vassal of the Sultan of Yola on the Benue, was also capturing slaves who were intended for commerce in Sokoto.

Thus throughout the 19th century the slave trade led to the systematic destruction of the population in northeast and east central Africa. Indeed, for more than 150 years slave taking and exportation was the main economic activity in the central African regions. Men were the only merchandise for the acquisition of arms and these arms were, in turn, used to capture more slaves. This vicious circle lasted until 1912, the date of the fall of Dar al-Kuti, the last slaving kingdom.

It is clear that the fear of capture for slavery forced the population to migrate and thus made it much easier for France to take possession of Central Africa. Although the information about the country's history at the time of the slave trade may be sketchy and limited to a few accounts collected by travellers in the country of Tekrour (notably Mohamed el Tounsy, Denham, Barth, Nachtigal), the period of Central African history beginning with the establishment of the first French posts is better known. The years during which France took responsibility for Central Africa, can be divided into several periods: exploration (before 1900); brutal exploitation (1900-20); attempts at colonization (1920-45); emancipation (1945-60); and the achievement of independence (after 1960).

The French government did not have sufficient financial means to organize expeditions to explore the area in the north of Gabon-Congo. This was done by a group of private individuals who had financed the Crampel expedition (which proposed to operate a link between Ubangi and Algeria, through a completely unknown country). After the assassination of Crampel and the destruction of his expedition in April 1891 by Muhammad as-Sanusi, the private individuals referred to above formed themselves into the 'Comité de l'Afrique française' to continue their explorations.

While Brazza's agents were establishing several posts in the Upper Ubangi in order to prevent Leopold II's agents from progressing towards the north, Brazza himself went to Upper Sangha to create posts and prevent the Germans from Cameroon from advancing towards the east. At the same time the Committee of French Africa was sending out a series of expeditions to take possession of the west and the centre of Central Africa, and to find a route of access to Chad (expeditions which were led by Dybowski, Maistre, Mizon and Clozel).

The passing of treaties and the founding of posts made it possible for France to secure the Upper Sangha and Upper Logone, the right bank of the Shari and the basin on the right bank of the Ubangi. In 1894, agreements made with Germany and King Leopold assured France of its domination in Central Africa that still continues today. In addition, France was now in a good position to dominante the countries situated on the right bank of the Shari. Moreover, these agreements led to the introduction of two projects, both of which seemed to be impracticable: the unification, desired by Paul Crampel, around Lake Chad of the French territories of North Africa, Senegal-Niger and Congo; and the French occupation of the Upper Nile, considered to be 'res nullius' since the Khedive of Egypt had renounced his rights over the Sudan. Two major expeditions, one led by Marchand and the other by Gentil, resulted.

Arriving on the Nile, in 1898 the French commander Jean-Baptiste Marchand did not find the Ethiopian military support promised by the Negus Menelik. He had to abandon the post of Fashoda to Great Britain's General Kitchener, who had been appointed by the Khedive of Egypt. This adventure brought about the French evacuation in 1899 of the posts established in the Bahr al-Ghazal. The failure of the Marchand mission caused the French to turn all their efforts toward the conquest of the Chad region.

In complete contrast to Marchand, Emil Gentil succeeded, in the area around Chad, in joining forces with expeditions from Alger and St Louis and in April 1900, he triumphed over Rabah. The fall of Rabah did not, however, assure the safety of the Central African populations, who were to suffer a series of new tragedies. As indicated above, Central Africa remained open to pro-slavery raids by Sanusi and the *lamido* of Ngaoundéré, and to tribal wars. The whole of the northeast of the country was abandoned to Muhammad as-Sanusi, Crampel's murderer, who had become France's protégé. The latter was to lead, with impunity, raids against the Banda and the Kreich in order to destroy and depopulate the region. Further south, the French tried to outlaw the traditional wars of Bangassou and Rafaï against the Banda. In the northwest of the country, Alphonse Goujon, the local administrator in charge of an army of several thousand Gbaya and Banda Yanguéré, forced the slave traders of the lamido of Ngaoundéré out of Central African territory in June 1896.

Between 1900 and the start of the First World War the history of Central Africa was characterised by a rather complex sequence of events. Even before occupying the territory, the French government divided the area belonging to the international Congo Basin into seventeen concessions and gave them up to private companies, each with enormous powers (1899). Under this system the Central African peoples were subjected to widespread exploitation and were forced to endure enormous injustices and privations. For example, the Manja people, decimated by porterage in which they were forced to participate, rose up in 1903. At about the same time, the populations of Lobaye and Upper Sangha, exasperated by the injustices committed by the agents from the companies, massacred several agents. Other native peoples were obliged to harvest rubber under atrocious conditions, whilst at the same time sleeping sickness and smallpox spread along the rivers claiming thousands of victims. As a result of these developments, Brazza, who had been dismissed in 1897, was recalled in 1905 to take charge of a tour of inspection. He was told to investigate the crimes committed by the companies' agents on the local populations in the Congo and Upper Shari. Brazza was surprised by the enormity of the crimes and his revelations, brought before the French Parliament in 1906, caused a scandal but did not lead to the abandonment of the concessionary system.

In 1906 Ubangi-Shari was united with Chad to form the French colony of Ubangi-Shari-Chad and in 1910 this became part of French Equatorial Africa. Thus, the whole of central Africa was placed under French administration. From 1909 to 1911 the French used military force to effectively reconquer what was now a ruined country. Meanwhile, Sanusi was denounced by the British for his transportation of slaves to Darfur. However, it was not until 1909, when the French made themselves master of Wadai (after a war lasting some ten years) that France's colonial administrators eventually decided to rid themselves of Sanusi, their cumbersome ally. On 11 January 1911 Sanusi and his son Adem were killed at the Ndélé post. Later that year on 4 November 1911 France gave up vast territories within French Equatorial Africa (which had only been created the previous year) to Germany, in exchange for recognition of its rights over Morocco. Thus the whole western part of present-day central Africa became German (Neu Kamerun).

Following the First World War, the territories given up in 1911 were returned to France and, in addition, it was given a mandate on the largest part of German Cameroon, which was occupied by French troops. France therefore found itself in charge of an immense area, stretching from the Tibesti desert, to the Congo and from the Atlantic to Bahr al-Ghazal.

The system of porterage had disappeared in Ubangi-Shari by 1920, thanks to the creation of a 4,200 kilometres network of roads by the governor, August Lamblin. He regrouped the villages along these roads. In addition, the administator, Félix Eboué, introduced the cultivation of cotton, with the purchasing of cotton being confined to French, Belgian and Dutch companies. Moreover, famine was relieved by the development of cultivated land beside the rivers based on a system of crop rotation. Plantations of the Excelsa coffee trees were also developed. In Upper Sangha, however, owing to a rise in the price of rubber, the concessionary companies started rubber harvesting again with the same brutality as before. Villagers were forced to accept unpaid work days and there was considerable labour unrest. The construction of the Congo-Ocean railway, moreover, necessitated the requisition of a large work-force mainly in Ubangi-Shari. Following the frightening death rate amongst the workers, the whole Gbaya population revolted in 1928, and they were soon followed by numerous other ethnic groups. This great colonial uprising, known as the Kongo Wara ('the war of the hoe-handle'), was to last almost three years. It led to the territory of Ubangi-Shari uniting with the basins of Lobaye and Upper Sangha, and the region of Bouar, which until this time had depended on Moyen-Congo. The revolt was ultimately suppressed and the years that followed saw the destruction of the Excelsa coffee plantations, instances of tracheo-mycosis, and the first effects of the world-wide economic crisis. In the Second World War the territory sided with Free France (1940). The Central Africans fought with the Free French, notably at the battle of Bir Hakeïm (May-June 1942) on the Libyan front. Félix Eboué, who knew Central Africa well, became the Governor General of Free French Africa in 1940. The new local policies, which he established in 1941, formed the basis for the imperial conference of Brazzaville in 1944, which was presided over by General de Gaulle and which considered France's colonial empire in Africa. This recommended the institution of a representative régime in overseas territories, while ruling out any system of self-government.

During the fifteen years following the Second World War Ubangi-Shari, along with other French territories of black Africa, moved towards autonomy, and then towards independence. The emancipa-tion of a territory which was still haunted by the ravages of its colonial past was carried out with severe problems, but without recourse to violence. The measures taken by France were: the abolition of forced labour; the setting up of an elected territorial assembly; the suppression of the system of 'benefits' and other forms of 'local government' exploitation; and the implementation of sound working practices involving real guarantees for paid workers. All these reforms, however, met with strong opposition on the part of the colonial society. The veterinary surgeon, René Malbrant, deputy for Ubangi-Shari-Chad, headed a movement in Paris, which rejected the first draft of the French Constitution which was accepted by parliament in 1946. This opposition movement proclaimed its attachment to the French Empire and its hostility to the reforms. In this same year, 1946, the Bangui Chamber of Commerce and Industry which was dominated by colonialists began a strike to protest against the abolition of forced labour. Notwithstanding this, funds from FIDES (Fonds d'Investissement pour le Développement Economique et Social) brought about a programme of public building and agricultural support, which Ubangi-Shari sorely needed.

As a result of Malbrant's campaign, Abbé Barthélemy Boganda, Central Africa's leading Catholic priest, who was elected Deputy of Ubangi-Shari on 10 November 1946 campaigned for equal rights for the French and the Central Africans. His talents brought him great popularity in a very few years, and his activities became known even in the most isolated villages. In spite of persecutions and electoral ploys, the party that he created in 1949 (MESAN, Mouvement pour l'Evolution Sociale de l'Afrique Noire), won all the elections. Elected successively deputy of Ubangi-Shari, mayor of Bangui and president of the 'Grand Conseil' of FEA, Barthélemy Boganda was considered in 1957, as the only worthwhile politician in the whole of the FEA.

The 'Loi Cadre' (Enabling Act), also called the Defferre Law, (23 June 1956) which opened the way for internal autonomy for the French overseas territories, came into force in Ubangi-Shari, and it soon met with difficulties. In May 1957, after being presented by Boganda, Doctor Abel Goumba was elected vice-president of the Council of Government, presided over by the French high commissioner. The following July Goumba became president of the Council of Government. Responsibility for administrative and economic affairs, was vested in one minister, a Frenchman, Roger Guérillot, who supported MESAN. Deeply disappointed by the refusal of the other territories to support the unity of French Equatorial Africa in the process of independence which had already taken place, Barthélemy Boganda accepted the presidency of a Central African Republic reduced to Ubangi-Shari. He was frightened by the huge costs involved in establishing and administering a new and overpopulated sovereign state, a state which he knew to be tragically lacking in administrative and technical staff and which had such a weak economy. Boganda suspected Roger Guérillot of conspiracy and decided to expel him from the government and send him to Paris as an exile.

Barthélemy Boganda was killed on 29 March 1959, when his aeroplane exploded, at a time when the Central African Republic had not yet attained independence. He was succeeded by David Dacko, who ousted Abel Goumba with the support of the French High Commissioner. Dacko awarded himself the title of President of the Republic on 14 August 1960, the day after the signing of the Act of Independence at Bangui. A few months later, he had laws voted in, restricting public freedom and arrested Abel Goumba and several anti-establishment deputies. In 1962 Dacko made MESAN the country's only political party and in 1964 he replaced the democratic constitution of 1959 with a new constitution, instituting a presidential system and a one-party-state. However, despite doubling taxes and instituting a system of obligatory withdrawal, Dacko could neither make up the deficit in the budget, nor stop the rapid deterioration of the economy. During the night of December 31-January 1 1966, he abandoned power to his Chief of Staff, Jean-Bedel Bokassa, a veteran of the colonial infantry, and Barthélemy Boganda's nephew.

Colonel Bokassa, who was to give himself the titles of General, Marshal, President for Life, then Emperor, plunged the country into total disaster during his bloody thirteen-year dictatorship. During these years the international community acted with complete indifference. Bokassa discredited the Central African élite, humiliated the population, and the splendours of his coronation ridiculed the country. Ultimately it was Amnesty International's denunciation of his personal participation in the massacre of children following the demonstration by school-children in January and April 1979, which was to lead to his downfall. Hoping to justify himself, he accepted the proposal made by the president of the French Republic, at the time of the Sixth Franco-African summit at Kigali, to form a commission of African magistrates charged with investigating the accusations. The commission's report was to be overwhelming. At the request of the Emperor's Prime Minister, Henri Maïdou, a French military operation (called Barracuda), put an end to this long and tragic masquerade. The French military did not encounter any opposition (20 September 1979) and Bokassa, who was turned away in France, found asylum in the Côte d'Ivoire. Meanwhile David Dacko, who had become political adviser to the Emperor, was brought back to the Central African Republic by French parachutists. Dacko immediately announced the return of the Republic and resumed his former post.

Helped by a team of French volunteers who tried to reorganize government adminstration and restore the economy, David Dacko retained power for less than two years. He failed in his attempt to restore an authoritarian regime and the new single-party state that he established met with failure. His government was weak financially, several of his ministers were imprisoned and the opposition was driven underground. In February 1981, however, he obtained the acceptance by referendum of a constitution that seemed to be democratic. The presidential elections that followed, however, only gave him a little more than fifty per cent of the votes, despite widespread vote rigging, and the late announcement of the results provoked serious incidents in the districts of Bangui. Amidst this confusion Bokassa's former prime minister, Ange Patassé, claimed power. In addition, the French presidential elections were a complete upset for David Dacko, who had been banking on the success of the former French president, Valéry Giscard d'Estaing, who had made him Head of State. As a result of these developments, on 1 September 1981, Dacko handed over power to his Head of Staff (General André Kolingba), as he had done fifteen years earlier. This transfer of power became known as the 'coup d'état by mutual agreement'.

Kolingba, Bokassa's former ambassador to Canada and West Germany, took steps to abolish the constitution. He took charge of a 'comité militaire de redressement national' (CMRN). The incompetence, corruption and tribalism that ruled within the junta in power was total. On March 3 1982, two members of the military committee attempted to seize power in a bid to support Ange Patassé. The conspiracy failed due to the rapid intervention of the presidential security forces, acting on the orders of the French Colonel Mantion. The French military contingent, sent to Central Africa to overthrow Bokassa's régime, had stayed on because of the situation in Chad. This contingent was renamed 'éléments français d'assistance opérationelle (EFAO)'. Reassured by the French military presence to which he owed his continued role as President, General Kolingba, however, showed himself to be hostile to any democratic reforms. In October 1986, under pressure from France, he nonetheless agreed to organize a referendum in order to adopt a presidential style of constitution, prepared by a French professor and including the necessary guarantees against any eventual coup d'état.

At about this time (23 October 1986), in a somewhat surprising turn of events, the ex-emperor Bokassa arrived at Bangui aerodrome, where he was arrested by Colonel Mantion. The Central African courts, with a lot of technical assistance from France, organized a public trial lasting several months, at the end of which (12 June 1987) the emperor was sentenced to death (a sentence confirming the death penalty pronounced in his absence on 20 December 1980). A few months later General Kolingba pardoned him and in 1991 his sentence was reduced to twenty years detention.

In July 1987 general elections were organized. This was the first time for twenty years that such elections had been held. The new assembly, however, was not to play a true role in public affairs, since it was still subjugated, as in the past, to the will of the president, who was also head of the only party.

There was deep unrest throughout the country because of the continual arrests of people who had committed 'crimes against the state' and because of the deteriorating economic situation. The embezzlement of public funds was increasing, though salaries were still paid albeit after long delays. Accordingly, it became necessary for France to pay exceptional budgetary subsidies. Moreover, the intervention of the International Monetary Fund necessitated the sacking of a certain number of civil servants.

Whilst Kolingba was trying to rebuild his single party (Rassemblement Démocratique Centrafricain, RDC), and to organize a single Central Union, 252 important people within the Republic sent an open letter to him, demanding the convening of a National Conference to discuss the serious crisis that affected the country (15 May 1990). This event led to numerous arrests, including Abel Goumba and the twenty-two main opponents of the government. The Committee for the Co-ordination of the Convening of the National Conference (CCCCN), was an organization formed from the union of various opposition movements, which had developed in secret. As a result of their actions, General Kolingba: released and granted amnesty to the majority of political prisoners; created the post of Prime Minister; made changes in his government; legalized the political parties; and accepted the need to hold a national conference but he failed to name a precise date. Nevertheless, faced with strike movements paralysing the country from May 1991 onwards, he took new repressive measures, including the suspension of union activities in the public sector and the imprisonment of the principal union leaders. As a result, the five Central African bishops sent a severe warning to the president of the Republic. Kolingba was constantly turning to France for help in order to avoid financial ruin. However, the French government exerted pressure on the Head of State in order to persuade him to take appropriate measures to ensure that his régime became truly democratic. Notwithstanding this, Kolingba, whose presidential mandate expired in 1992, kept postponing the process of democratisation.

Central African Republic Institutions

During the last thirty years, the Central African Republic has been governed by some eight constitutions. They have all been drawn up by professors of French law, all have been theoretical, and all have been violated by successive Heads of State, who had taken oaths pledging to respect them.

The first constitution was promulgated on 15 February 1959, at a time when the country had not yet attained full sovereignty. The Central African Republic, a member state of the French Community composed of France and its overseas territories, was initially given democratic institutions, inspired by those of France. President Barthélemy Boganda had been anxious that the written constitution should be preceded by an introduction guaranteeing the exercise of complete public freedom. He also added an article to the constitution which allowed for the transfer of the rights of sovereignty of the new State to a larger whole.

All the subsequent constitutions had a common trait: measures were violated and then legalized; and the author of these violations, with adequate legal help from French experts, would then be granted supreme power. For four years, the country was governed by a constitution voted for by the legislative assembly which had been elected before independence, thus distorting the constitution of 15 February 1959, notably by restricting the exercise of public freedom. On 19 November 1963, a bizarre constitutional law was passed which allowed for the election, by universal suffrage, for a seven-year mandate, of a sole candidate for the presidency of the Republic, chosen by a single party. David Dacko was elected in this way, with an overwhelming majority, on 20 November 1964. He replaced the existing constitution with a new text which gave official backing to a severe presidential regime. Through the intervention of a management committee from MESAN, David Dacko was provided with wide powers. In the same month (November) 1964, the president of the Republic decided to create a 'vigilance committee' in each sub-prefecture, made up of members of MESAN. They were responsible for resolving the numerous difficulties which had arisen between the civil servants in authority and the citizens. By subsequently abandoning all his power to Colonel Jean-Bedel Bokassa on 1 January 1966, David Dacko violated the constitution of 1964.

The officers involved in the coup d'état of 1966 created a revolutionary council which replaced the Council of Ministers. Two constitutional acts of 4 and 8 January 1966, which were written up in the Vichy model, entrusted all the executive and legislative power to the Head of State. It was not until ten years later, after having survived an attempt on his life on 3 February 1976, that the Central African dictator, now life-president, convened a party congress, which conferred on him the title of Emperor. In 1979, the advisers to the president of the French Republic suggested unsuccessfully that the Emperor should abdicate and organize a regency. Since this was not accepted by Bokassa, France by military intervention organized the reinstatement of the former president, David Dacko on 20 September 1979. He was careful not to re-establish the constitution that he had violated on 1 January 1966.

This Republic was to last for less than two years. A constitutional act of 21 September 1979 established a provisional re-organization of departments. After several attempts at reorganizing the governmental team and restoring the single-party system, the president, David Dacko, reluctantly proposed an amendment to the constitution which allowed for a multi-party system of government, and presidential elections consisting of several candidates (1 February 1981). The troubled situation continued after the presidential elections when David Dacko won by an extremely narrow margin, and the amendments were not brought into force. As he had already done on 1 January 1966, David Dacko handed all of his power back to his Head of Staff (1 September 1981), once again in violation of his country's constitution.

For more than five years, just as Jean-Bedel Bokassa had done fifteen years earlier, General André Kolingba, claimed complete executive and legislative power, and tried to institute a new single party, after having repealed the constitutional amendments.

This republic remained constitutionally exposed and the French experts again had to provide it with a legal framework. A few days after the opening of ex-Emperor Bokassa's trial, the President-General presented a new constitutional text, to be approved by the Central Africans (21 November 1986). This text, affirmed 'the firm will of the Central African people to develop a State of Law'. The Central African people were, however, asked to reply 'yes' or 'no' in a ballot, to the adoption of this text and to the regularization of the role of the President (Kolingba). The latter found himself elected president of the Republic for a seven-year mandate, renewable by referendum at his own initiative. The year before, he had dissolved the 'Comité militaire de Redressement National' (CMRN), formed in September 1981, and had replaced it with a government made up of some civilian ministers.

A bicameral system, in appearance only, was established; Parliament consisted of a National Assembly and an Economic and Regional Council. The composition of this second assembly was as follows: half of its members were appointed by the President, and half of its members were elected by the national assembly, nominated by its president. It served in a purely advisory capacity. However, the two assemblies meeting in Congress could pass basic laws, and laws revising the constitution, when they were not subject to a referendum. The responsibility for making the laws was shared between the President of the Republic and a third of the deputies making up the National Assembly. A supreme court (Court of Appeal and Constitutional Council) was also set up.

In fact, the principal aim of these constitutional arrangements was to prevent another coup d'état. A High Court of Justice consisting of nine judges (three chosen by the President of the Republic, three by the President of Congress and three by the President of the Supreme Court) was also established. This high court had the power to try not only members of the government and of Congress, but anybody guilty of conspiracy, attemped conspiracy or even of any act involving 'intelligence', whatever it may be, concerning foreign powers, presumed to be oposed to the State's interests. To assure the continuance of this system General André Kolingba tried, like his predecessors, to institute a single party.

The proclamation of a State of Law did not, however, prevent the General-President from banning all political activity in the country and from arresting numerous opponents. Nonetheless, when asked by his supporters to democratize his regime, General André Kolingba had to make several modifications to the constitution. He was forced to appoint a prime minister; to institute a multi-party system (the parties remaining, however, were subject to his authorization); and to stop condemning prisoners of conscience, who had been detained for many months. As a result, in April 1991, he pronounced an amnesty for the majority of these prisoners although the difficult economic and social situation served as a pretext which enabled him to put off indefinitely the formation of a national conference which had been called for by the opposition.

During 1992 General Kolingba had to face almost permanent strikes and the salaries of the civil servants were not paid for months on end. Whilst the opposition demanded a national conference on sovereignty, the Head of State was organising a national debate, in which most of his opponents refused to take part. On 7 September Kolingba agreed to set the date for the first round of the presidential and legislative elections for the 25 October. As the first results showed that the four other candidates for the presidency were leading the president, Kolingba suspended the poll in Bangui and then had the whole electoral process cancelled by the constitutional council on 29 October.

Kolingba's mandate expired on 28 November 1992 but he decided to remain in power by means of a 'constitutional coup d'état'. He invoked Article 13 of the constitution which he did not have the legal power to put into force and decided to extend his functions as president for 90 days. On 4 December he nominated General Malendoma, an opponent, as Prime Minister and an order set the date of the presidential and legislative elections for 14 and 28 February 1993. On 3 February he set up an interim authority 'Le Conseil national politique provisoire de la République' (CNPPR) – the Provisional National Political Council of the Republic. This comprised, besides Kolingba himself, three other candidates in the presidential elections: David Dacko, the former president of the Republic; Ange Patassé, Emperor Bokassa's previous Prime Minister; and Enoch Derant-Lakoué, the former finance minister of the imperial government. Professor Abel Goumba, the leader of the CFD (Concertation des Forces Démocratiques) – The Democratic Force for Dialogue – refused to join the 'bande des quatre' (the gang of four), a name given by the people to the provisional government. Goumba announced the deposition of the General President as of 28 February 1993.

General Kolingba dismissed Prime Minister Timothée Malendoma on 25 February and provided Enoch Derant-Lakoué the task of forming another government. He postponed the forthcoming elections firstly to the 18 April and 2 May of then to the 30 May and 13 June. This rejection of the process of democratisation, parallelled by the behaviour of Marshal President Mobutu in Zaire, served to increase political unrest. On 26 April 1993 the police forcefully quelled a demonstration in the streets of Bangui organised by civil servants, students and schoolchildren; two people were killed and forty-five injured. On 29 April 1993 the government announced yet another postponement of the elections to the 17th and 31st October 1993.

Economy

Central Africa possesses a huge potential for wealth. It is the location of Africa's best humid savannas, which are suitable for cultivation and for animal breeding. None of the populated regions is over-populated and ore and mineral deposits are plenty. Its dense forest is one of the richest in the world, and until now has been relatively protected. Yet the Central African Republic is listed amongst the least-advanced countries and amongst those who depend the most on foreign aid. Known to the world for barely a century, Central Africa is still far from participating in the world market economy.

Until about 1925, the only things to come out of this country were slaves, ivory and raw rubber, and these were extracted under the appalling conditions with which we are now familiar. From 1925 to 1940, the colonizers imposed the obligatory cultivation of cotton and, just before the Second World War, Ubangi-Shari was the main producer of cotton in the French Empire. A large part of the export receipts from this product were, incidentally, used to undertake public building programmes in the rest of French Equatorial Africa. From 1940 to 1960, while maintaining the widespread cultivation of cotton, the authorities also ensured the development of coffee production (industrial plantations and, just before independence, family plantations), and the production of gold and diamonds. In addition, the exploitation of the forests was intensified in order to boost exports. At present these four products still make up the country's main exports.

During the period between 1940 and 1960 the obligatory cultivation of cotton, throughout the whole country gave an annual production of around 30,000 tons of cotton-seeds. During the last three decades, production has held steady at around this figure, peaking between 1968 and 1970 at more than 50,000 tons and during periods of poor growth falling to less than 20,000 tons. Cotton cultivation now covers an area of less than 60,000 hectares and productivity is around 650 kilogrammes a hectare. The equipment is still very rudimentary and only a third of the land is improved by fertilizers or insecticides. Moreover, the attempts at animal drawn cultivation have not produced the expected results.

In 1960, family cultivation of Robusta coffee trees was still few and far between, and the national production of about 6,000 tons of coffee for the market came from essentially European plantations. The subsequent rapid development of production led to the imposition of quotas of 9,000, then 12,000 tons, on the Central African Republic by the 'Accord International du Café'. At present, coffee trees cover a little more than 34,000 hectares consisting mainly of small family plantations. Having at one time exceeded 18,000 tons, production is holding steady at around 12,000 tons of very high quality coffee which is exported to France and Italy.

Diamond production, which is now clearly the most important export, is the work of numerous artisans, who sell the diamonds to buying offices which export them mainly to Antwerp. A small number of stones are cut in Bangui in a national diamond cutting factory created in 1965 by the Central African government in a joint venture with an American company, to which the main buying office belongs. Before 1962, production was assured only be foreign companies with mining rights. In 1954, production exceeded 150,000 carats but current production is higher and fluctuates at around 400,000 carats. In addition, between 200 and 400 kilos of gold is produced (in 1934 it was nearer 1 ton). This small-scale local production is, however, not without its drawbacks. It has led to the abandonment of numerous enterprises and, because it is carried out with no methodical prospecting, it has jeopardized the later, more rational mining activities. The establishment of rice-fields in the rivers, using heavy equipment, which was envisaged around 1965, has not materialised.

Timber exports have, over the last twenty years, supplemented exports of coffee, cotton and diamonds. Taking into account the enormous problems of transport, this export has never exceeded the 100,000 cubic metres of unprocessed and sawed wood which was reached in 1970. In 1990, exports were limited to 64,890 cubic metres of unprocessed wood and 30,628 cubic metres of sawed wood.

It was hoped that substantial extra revenue would come from the development of sisal (2,000 tons exported in 1945), of hevea rubber (1,000 tons exported in 1969), of tobacco (2,000 tons in the 1970s) and of other products. However, insufficient investment was made in the production of these crops and they have either disappeared, or have seriously declined. Various initiatives in other directions initially produced satisfactory results (cocoa-plants, pepper-plants, cola-plants, mulberry trees etc. . . .), but these successes were not maintained. The plan to mine uranium in the Bakouma region (1,000 tons of metal uranium) has also been dropped. Moreover, food production (estimated at half a million tons of manioc, a hundred thousand tons of groundnuts, and consequential tonnages of sesame, millet, gourd seeds), thanks notably to the ease with which manioc can be grown and to its huge yield, provides food for the rural populations and the urban areas, which are already supplied with fresh produce by the urban plantations. Due to the increase in the herds reared by the Mbororo, the Central African Republic curently has as many head of cattle as inhabitants. Moreover, every village or town has a large number of pigs, goats, sheep and poultry.

The industrial sector represents less than 10 per cent of the Gross National Product. All that it consists of now is some modest factories, carrying out the processing of primary products and assembly functions, all concentrated in Bangui. Breweries and cigarette factories are also thriving. Numerous projects in many sectors have been abandoned because of the small national market and the lack of organization of the common market that should make up the UDEAC (Union Douanière et Economique de l'Afrique Centrale), which united the four states of former French Equatorial Africa (Chad, Gabon, Congo and the Central African Republic) and the Federal Republic of Cameroon.

Various economic indicators reveal the extent of under-development. The production of electricity was still, in 1990, less than 100 million kilowatt hours (it was five times less than this figure in 1964). The number of people with electricity has only just exceeded 7,000. The number of people who have running water is about the same and the number with a telephone (including those involved in the administration of the country) is around 6,000. The country only imports some 90,000 cubic metres of petroleum products of all kinds (including paraffin oil and aviation fuel). Bangui's river port monopolizes the majority of imports and exports and continues to provide part of the imports and exports of Chad. The inland road network totals 23,728 kilometres, of which 5,398 kilometres are main roads (only 440 kilometres are asphalted). Almost all of the air traffic is centred on the aerodrome of Bangui-M'Poko and communications with neighbouring countries are of little importance.

Taking into account the weakness of export revenue, the poor revenue from tax, fraud on customs dues and, above all, poor administrative management and the extent of embezzlement of public funds, the budgetary deficit is currently more than 40 billion francs CFA. The national debt is almost 200 billion francs CFA, in spite of deferments.

The structural imbalance of public finances, the disequilibrium of the balance of payments and the burden of the national debt, have forced the Central African Republic to seek financial aid from the International Monetary Fund, which has imposed a batch of stabilization measures. Among them is the obligation to reduce the number of civil servants and police, which increased from 6,000 in the first years of independence, to some 26,000. The payment of public salaries alone, although frozen since 1981, would absorb more than eighty-five per cent of the budget receipts which, accordingly, have to be supplemented by 'budgetary grants'. The state, by far the largest employer, was forced to delay any new appointments and a tense social situation has naturally resulted. The total work-force employed in skilled jobs, i.e., employed in the so-called modern sector, did not exceed 24,000 in 1990, more than 6,000 of whom worked in private services. The official statistics include another so-called informal sector, composed of 30,000 people, including about 25,000 tradesmen and pedlars.

It is certain that the 'Balkanization' of French Equatorial Africa has seriously jeopardized the economic development of the Central African Republic which has such a small population and is land-locked. Like Boganda, the agronomist René Dumont considers that only a union of territory stretching from Douala to Rwanda, could have formed a viable economic unit. Central Africa, because of the absence of sufficient access roads, suffers from bad trading links more than any other country in the region. Even the project to link up with the Trans-Cameroon railway has been abandoned, in order to improve and extend the road links towards the West.

On the other hand, aid programmes likely to improve the infrastructure and basic public services have been neglected, in favour of the relatively ineffective direct aid designed to help export production.

Statistics show a total of 4,052 beds for the sick, only 1,283 of which are real hospital beds, with a total staff in the health sector, both public and private, of 3,918 people, nationals and foreigners. The number of Central African doctors barely exceeds one hundred, to which about forty foreign doctors can be added.

In 1962, state and private education was unified. The total number of pupils has increased since then from 90,000 to more than 370,000 today, 40,000 of whom are in secondary education. From 1987 to 1990, however, the number of primary school teachers was reduced by one thousand (from 4,563 to 3,581). Technical education still only has 3,500 pupils and Bangui University, after a quarter of a century of existence, only has a little more than 3,000 students.

It is obvious that the introduction of a programme based on health and education would have a profound effect on the economic and social development of the country. There are programmes of this kind 'at village level' but they are still in the experimental stage. In this crucial era of social change, only the Christian missions (500,000

Introduction

Catholics, 400,000 Protestants) currently provide well-established structures. The insufficient administration of the rural zones, and the rural exodus towards Bangui and the urban zones are becoming more pronounced and the situation remains, tragically, beyond remedy.

Abbreviations and Acronyms

ACCT	Agence de Coopération Culturelle et Technique (The Agency for Cultural and Technical Cooperation)
AEF	Afrique Equatoriale Française (French Equatorial Africa)
AMAROM	Association des amis des archives d'Outre-Mer (The Association of Friends for Overseas Archives)
BCEOM	Bureau Central d'Etudes pour les Equipements d'Outre-Mer (The Central Bureau for Overseas Equipment)
BDPA	Bureau pour le Développement de la Production Agricole (The Bureau for the Development of Agricultural Production)
BEAC	Banque Centrale des Etats de l'Afrique Centrale (The Central Bank of the Central African States)
BRGM	Bureau de Recherches Géologiques et Minières (The Bureau of Geological and Mining Research)
CAR	Central African Republic
CCCCN	Comité de Coordination pour la Convocation d'une Conférence Nationale (The Coordinating Committee for the Convening of a National Congress)
CCCE	Caisse Centrale de Coopération Economique (The Central Bank for Economic Cooperation)
CFA	Communauté Financière Africaine (The African Financial Community) (1 franc CFA = 2 centimes français)
CFDT	Campagnie Française pour le Développement des Fibres Tropicaux (The French Company for the Development of Tropical Fibres)

Abbreviations and Acronyms

CHEAM	Centre des Hautes Etudes sur l'Afrique et l'Asie Modernes (The Centre for Higher Research on Modern Africa and Asia)
CIRAD	Centre de Coopération Internationale en Recherches Agronomiques pour le Développement (The Centre for International Cooperation in Agricultural Research and Development)
CLEF	Cercle des lecteurs d'Expression Française (The Circle of French-Speaking Readers)
CMRN	Comité Militaire de Redressement National (The Military Committee for National Recovery)
CRET	Centre de Recherches d'Etudes Tropicales (The Research Centre for Tropical Studies)
CTFT	Centre Technique Forestier Tropical (The Technical Centre for Tropical Forestry)
CUP	Cambridge University Press
EFAO	Eléments Français d'Assistance Opérationnelle (French Unit for Military Aid)
EPHE	Ecole Pratique des Hautes Etudes (The Higher Research Institute)
FEA	French Equatorial Africa
FIDES	Fonds d'Investissement pour le Développement Economique et Social (The Investment Fund for Economic and Social Development)
IGN	Institut Géographique National (National Geographical Institute)
INALCO	Institut National des Langues et Civilisations Orientales (The National Institute for Oriental Languages and Civilisations)
IRCC	Institut de Recherches sur le Café et le Cacao (The Coffee and Cocoa Research Institute)
LACITO	Laboratoire des Langues et Civilisations à Traditions Orales (The Laboratory for Languages and Civilisations with Oral Traditions)
MESAN	Mouvement pour l'Evolution Sociale de l'Afrique Noire (Movement for social evolution in Black Africa)
MNHN	Muséum National d'Histoire Naturelle (The National Natural History Museum)

MRP	Maitre de Recherches Principal (ORSTOM) (The Head of Research (in ORSTOM))
MSH	Maison des Sciences de l'Homme (The Museum of Human Sciences)
OECD	Organisation for Economic Cooperation and Development
ONUDI	Organisation des Nations Unies pour le Développement Industriel (The UN Organisation for Industrial Development)
ORSTOM	Office de la Recherche Scientifique et Technique d'Outre-Mer (The Office for Scientific & Technical Research Overseas)
PUF	Presses Universitaires de France (French University Press)
RCA	République Centrafricaine (The Central African Republic)
RDC	Rassemblement Démocratique Centrafricain (The Central African Democratic Union)
SEDES	Société d'Etudes pour le Développement Economique et Social (The Society for the Study of Economic and Social Development)
SELAF	Société d'Etudes Linguistiques et Anthropologiques de France (The French Society for Linguistic and Anthropological Study)

Chronology

1889 25 June	The foundation of the post at Bangui by Alfred Uzac and Michel Dolisie.
1890–1894	Various French expeditions reach the Central African territory via Benue, Sangha and Ubangi. The establishment of the first administrative posts.
1891–1894	Agents of the independent state of the Congo establish posts to the north of Mbomou.
1894 13 February	The foundation of the St. Paul Mission in Bangui by Father Prosper Augouard.
1894 15 March	The Franco-German Convention settles the border between Cameroon and the French Congo.
1894 13 July	The Decree establishing the French territory of Upper Ubangi.
1894 14 August	The Franco-Leopoldian agreement which establishes the Northern border of the independent state of the Congo in the valley of the Mbomou.
1897 1 November	The explorer Emil Gentil reaches the shores of Lake Chad.
1897–1899	French posts are established in Bahr al-Ghazal.
1898 10 July	The Congo-Nile expedition, led by Captain Jean-Baptiste March and arrives at Fashoda on the Nile.
1899 21 March	An Anglo-French agreement settles the border between the Sudan and the Congo, at the watershed of the Congo and Nile rivers.

1899	The French government allows concessionary companies to operate in more than 75 per cent of the Central African territory.
1900 22 April	Rabah is defeated and killed by the French in Kousseri.
1902–1904	The Mandja rebellion.
1903 29 December	The decree creating the colony of Ubangi-Shari.
1902–1905	The Lobaye uprising.
1906 11 February	The establishment of the colony of Ubangi-Shari-Chad and its capital Fort de Possel.
1906 11 December	A decree making Bangui the capital of Ubangi-Shari-Chad.
1909–1911	A general uprising of the Central African people and the reconquest of the country by the French.
1910 15 January	The French Congo becomes French Equatorial Africa (FEA) when the colonies of Gabon, Middle-Congo, Ubangi-Shari and Chad all join together.
1911 4 November	France cedes to Germany a large part of French Equatorial Africa and in particular the Western part of present-day Central Africa. The annexe territories are called Neu Kamerun.
1914 August-December	The French re-occupy Neu Kamerun and enter German Cameroon.
1928–1931	A general uprising of the Gbaya and other groups in the western part of Central Africa known as the 'Kongo-Wara' war.
1940 3 September	Ubangi-Shari rallies to the side of the Free French.
1944 30 January	General de Gaulle opens the Brazzaville conference on the future of the French African Empire.
1946 16 October	The administrative reorganisation of French Equatorial Africa into four regions.

Chronology

1946 10 November	Barthélemy Boganda was elected Deputy for Ubangi-Shari in the French National Assembly.
1947 March-December	The Territorial Assembly of Ubangi-Shari and the Grand Council of the AEF are established.
1949 28 September	Barthélemy Boganda establishes the Movement for Social Evolution in Black Africa (MESAN).
1951 10 January	Boganda and his wife are arrested.
1951 17 June	Boganda is re-elected to the French National Assembly (despite strong opposition).
1952 30 March	MESAN takes all the seats in the Ubangi-Shari territorial assembly.
1954 30 April-1 May	The Berbérati riot (following the death of a domestic servant and his wife in the service of a French official known for his brutal treatment of the Africans).
1956 2 January	Boganda is re-elected to the French National Assembly.
1956 28 November	Boganda is elected Mayor of Bangui.
1957 17 May	The first Ubangian government is established, directed by Doctor Abel Goumba.
1957 18 June	Boganda is elected President of the Grand Council of the FEA.
1958 28 September	Ubangui-Shari votes overwhelmingly (98.1%) in favour of continuing within the French community. Boganda recommends an independent Republic made up of the countries belonging to the FEA as the first step in the creation of a United States of Latin Africa.
1958 1 December	An independent Central African Republic is proclaimed, its territory limited to Ubangi-Shari. Boganda becomes President.
1959 16 February	The territorial Assembly adopts a democratic constitution presented by Boganda.
1959 29 March	Barthélemy Boganda is killed in a plane crash. Abel Goumba becomes interim president.

1959 5 May	David Dacko is elected President.
1960 13 August	The Central African Republic gains independence. David Dacko becomes Head of State.
1960 20 September	The Central African Republic is admitted to the United Nations.
1960 17 November	Demonstrations in Bangui against laws restricting public liberties.
1960 23 December	The arrest of Abel Goumba and several other members of The Movement for the Democratic Evolution of Central Africa (MEDAC) which is disbanded.
1962 22 February	Abel Goumba is convicted for provoking unlawful assembly.
1963 May	The National Assembly makes MESAN the country's only political party to which all citizens are obliged to belong.
1964 5 January	David Dacko, the only candidate, is elected President of the Republic by 99.99% of the vote.
1964 20 November	The passing of the constitution to create a presidental regime and the single party system.
1966 1 January	David Dacko is arrested by the military and hands over his power to Colonel Jean-Bedel Bokassa, the army Chief of Staff.
1966 4 January	The Abolition of the 1964 Constitution and the passing of the constitutional acts which establish a dictatorship.
1969 12 April	Lieutenant Colonel Alexandre Banza, the principal agent of the military coup d'état of 1966, was arrested, accused of conspiracy, was tortured and shot.
1972 4 May	General Bokassa is made life President.
1974 20 May	General Bokassa is nominated Marshal.

Chronology

1975 6–7 March	The French President Valéry Giscard d'Estaing presides over the Franco-African conference in Bangui.
1976 3 February	A grenade attack on Bokassa at Bangui airport. The arrest and execution of those involved in the conspiracy in the days following.
1976 5 September	The Council of Ministers is renamed the Revolutionary Council. Ange Patassé becomes Prime Minister.
1976 17 September	David Dacko is released from prison and appointed political adviser to the Head of State.
1976 October	Colonel Ghadafi, Libyan Head of State, visits Bangui.Bokassa announces his conversion to Islam.
1976 4 December	Bokassa renounces Islam and becomes the Emperor of Central Africa at an extraordinary congress of MESAN.
1977 4 December	Bokassa's coronation in Bangui.
1977 6 December	American aid to the country is suspended.
1979 17–22 January	Student demonstrations in Bangui are stopped with much bloodshed. The students were demonstrating against the wearing of obligatory uniforms sold in Bokassa's stores.
1979 18–19 April	Renewed demonstrations. Bokassa is involved in the massacre of approximately 100 demonstrators aged between 8 and 16 years of age.
1979 14 May	Amnesty International reveals and denounces the massacres committed at Bangui.
1979 21–22 May	At the Franco-African summit in Kigali, Bokassa accepts a commission of inquiry, made up of 5 African jurists, set up by President Valéry Giscard d'Estaing, to look into the massacre at Bangui.
1979 17 August	French aid is suspended, except for those activities which directly affect the life of the people.

1979 20–21 September	Whilst Bokassa is on a trip to Libya, French parachutists seize the airport and city of Bangui. This operation takes place at night and there is no resistance.
1979 21 September	David Dacko arrives in Bangui from Paris with a contingent of French troops and proclaims the re-establishment of the Republic. He announces that he is taking over his former functions as president of the Republic. Henri Maidou, Bokassa's prime minister, is nominated vice-president of the Republic. It was he who had asked for French intervention.
1979 24 September	Bokassa asks for asylum in France. He is eventually given refuge in the Ivory Coast.
1979 24 October	Ange Patassé is arrested in Bangui on his return from France via Libya.
1980 4 January	Dacko abolishes the right to strike.
1980 February	The formation of a new party, the Central African Democratic Union (UDC). This was the only political party which was permitted.
1980 17 July	Bernard-Christian Ayandho becomes Prime Minister.
1980 19 November	Jean-Pierre Lebouder becomes Prime Minister.
1980 8–14 December	Dacko organises a seminar of national reflection.
1980 24 December	Bokassa is sentenced to death in his absence.
1980 27 December	Dacko recognises political parties again.
1981 1 February	A new constitution is adopted as the result of a referendum with 97.3% of the votes cast in favour.
1981 March	Abel Goumba returns to Bangui after 19 years in exile.

Chronology

1981 15 March	Dacko is elected president with a very narrow majority (50.23% of the votes). There is an outbreak of violence when the results are announced.
1981 3 April	Simon Narcisse Bozanga becomes Prime Minister.
1981 14 July	A bomb explosion in a cinema in Bangui claims four lives and 32 injured. A few days later Rodolphe Iddi-Lala, the founder of a small group called the Central African Movement for National Liberation (MCLN), claims responsibility for the attack.
1981 10 August	Dacko prohibits opposition parties.
1981 1 September	Dacko hands over power to General André Kolingba, Head of the Army Chiefs of Staff.
1981 2 September	Kolingba suspends the constitution and creates a military committee for national recovery (CMRM).
1982 3 March	The failure of an attempted putsch by Bozizé, Marboua and Mbaikoua, army generals close to Ange Patassé.
1982 8 March	Ange Patassé takes refuge in the French Embassy in Bangui.
1982 13 April	A French military plane takes Ange Patassé to Togo.
1982 22 August	Abel Goumba, the President and founder of the Ubangui Patriotic Front – Labour Party (FPO/PT) and rector of Bangui University, is arrested, together with his assistant Patrice Endjimoungou.
1982 10 December	An international committee to support political prisoners in the Central African Republic is founded in Paris.
1983 1 September	Abel Goumba and 64 political prisoners are freed.

l

1983 4 December	Bokassa arrives in France and goes to live in his castle (Château de Hardricourt) not far from Paris.
1984 26 January	Abel Goumba, Henri Maidou and several other opposition leaders are arrested. Student unrest.
1984 31 January	The university and all schools in Bangui are closed.
1984 9–10 November	The Markounda outpost at the border with Chad is attacked by supporters of Ange Patassé.
1984 12–13 November	The French President, François Mitterrand pays an official visit to Bangui.
1984 31 December	Abel Goumba and 43 political prisoners are freed.
1985 13 February	Francois Guéret, Dacko's former Minister of Justice, is arrested on his return from Paris and accused of conspiracy.
1986 27 March	A Jaguar French military airplane crashes on a school in a heavily-populated area of Bangui. At least 35 people are killed and many are injured, most of them children. Anti-French protests follow.
1986 May	Schools and the university strike.
1986 7 May	Kolingba creates a new single-party state based on his new political organization, The Central African Democratic Assembly (RDC).
1986 23 October	Bokassa returns to Bangui and is arrested at the airport by the French Colonel Jean-Claude Mantion.
1986 21 November	A new constitution is adopted. Presidential elections take place. Kolingba, the only candidate, is elected President for a 6-year term of office.
1987 12 June	Following a public trial lasting 90 days, Bokassa is condemned to death by the Criminal Court in Bangui.

1987 July	The first legislative elections for 23 years.
1988 29 February	Kolingba commutes the death sentence passed on Bokassa to life imprisonment.
1989 5 January	Edouard Franck becomes Minister of State in charge of ministerial appointments.
1989 1 September	General François Bozizé and 11 of his supporters are arrested in Contonou in Benin and brought to Bangui to face imprisonment.
1990 15 May	600 people sign a petition asking Kolingba to open a national conference. The signatories are arrested.
1990 12 September	Abel Goumba and 22 other opposition members in charge of the coordinating committee for the convocation of a national conference (CCCCN) are arrested.
1990 9 October	The lawyer, Nicolas Tangaye, is prosecuted for siding with the opposition.
1990 13–15 October	Riots in Bangui. The arrest of General Timothée Malendoma, a former minister.
1991	Lengthy strikes by the public services.
1991 4 March	Kolingba frees Abel Goumba and the 22 opposition members arrested in September 1990.
1991 15 March	Edouard Franck becomes Prime Minister.
1991 22 April	Kolingba announces the return to a multi-party system.
1991 5 May	Abel Goumba's Ubangi Patriotic Front/Labour Party (FPV/PT) becomes the Patriotic Front for Progress (FPP).
1991 20 June	In a pastoral letter, the Central African Episcopal Conference asks for a national plan for recovery.
1991 3 July	The army occupies the Labour Exchange in Bangui.

1991 1 December	General François Bozizé is freed (after his acquittal on 24 September).
1992 13 February	20 opposition parties form a United Force for Central African Democracy (CFDC) to demand a national conference on sovereignty.
1992 1 August	Kolingba opens the Great National Debate. Political parties and trade unions refuse to participate. There are disturbances in Bangui during which Doctor Jean-Claude Conjugo, one of the leaders of the Alliance for Democracy and Progress (ADP), is killed by the police.
1992 7 September	A decree sets the date of the legislative and presidential elections for 25 October.
1992 25 October	The first round of presidential and legislative elections. They were badly organised, the ballot was suspended in Bangui. The results from the provinces indicated that Kolingba had been badly beaten.
1992 29 October	The Supreme Court annuls the elections.
1992 28 November	Despite the fact that his mandate has expired, Kolingba decides to continue in power.
1992 4 December	General Timothée Malendoma is nominated Prime Minister.
1992 28 December	The new dates for elections are fixed for 14 and 18 February.
1993 3 February	General Kolingba sets up an interim organisation called the 'Conseil National Politique Provisoire de la République (CNPPR) – the Provisional National Political Council of the Republic. This includes, as well as himself, three of the other candidates in the presidential elections: David Dacko, the former President of the Republic; Ange Patassé, the former Prime Minister; and Enoch Lakoué, the former Minister of Finance under Emperor Bokassa. The date of the elections are postponed to 18 April and 2 May.
1993 26 February	General Timothée Malendoma is sacked and replaced as Prime Minister by Enoch Lakoué.

1993 28 February	Professor Abel Goumba, the leader of the 'Concertation des Forces Democratiques' (CFD) – The Democratic Force for Dialogue, who refused to be involved in the provisional government, proclaims that Kolingba was no longer President as of 28 February.
1993 26 April	Demonstrations in Bangui by schoolchildren, students and civil servants against the government. Police intervention causes 2 deaths and 45 people are injured.
1993 29 April	The elections are again postponed. The government announces that they will take place 17 and 31 October.
1993 15 May	A mutiny by the Presidential guard composed mainly of the Yakoma (the same tribe as the President) and commanded by a French colonel.
1993 20 May	The creation of the UFAC (the Union of the Forces For Change) which united almost all of the opposition parties. A mutiny by the RDOT (the Regiment For The Operational Defence of the Territory) and part of the police force. These mutinies are caused because pay and allowances have not been paid for eight months. The mutineers receive two months' salary on account.
1993 4 June	Five thousand women hold a demonstration in Bangui. The gathering is dispersed when shots are fired.
1993 5 June	Michel Roussin, the French Minister for Cooperation, makes a lightning visit to Bangui. Colonel Jean-Claude Mantion, President Kolingba's special adviser and the ambassador, Alain Pallu de Beaupuy, are recalled to France. The Minister asks Kolingba to put forward to July the elections scheduled for October.
1993 6 June	A meeting between Kolingba and Mobutu in Gbadolité in Zaire.

The Country and Its People

1 **L'Afrique Equatoriale Française. Le pays, les habitants, la colonisation, les pouvoirs publics.** (French Equatorial Africa: the country, the people, colonization and the government.)
Georges Bruel. Paris: Larose, 1918. 558p. maps. bibliog.
The author was one of the earliest colonial administrators in the French colony of Ubangi-Shari. His book represents the sum of knowledge available at that time on the four territories of French Equatorial Africa created in 1910. It contains especially detailed notes about the various Central African peoples at the beginning of the colonial period: river peoples, forest peoples, and savanna peoples.

2 **La République Centrafricaine.** (The Central African Republic.)
Gérard Grellet, Monique Mainguet, Pierre Soumille. Paris: PUF, 1982. 128p. (Que Sais-Je, no. 1943).
A geographer, a geologist and an historian are the authors of this small volume which is divided into three parts which present: a study of the physical environment (geology and geography); historical data; and brief economic and demographic information. The book is a useful introduction to the study of the country.

3 **Afrique Equatoriale Française.** (French Equatorial Africa.)
Edited by Charles Guernier. Paris: Encyclopédie de l'Union Française, Editions de l'Encyclopédie Coloniale et Maritime, 1950. 590p. maps. bibliog.
This work was published under the auspices of the government of French Equatorial Africa. It consists of excellent articles written by experts on the country at that time, notably by the directors of the administrative and technical services of the colony.

4 **La République Centrafricaine.** (The Central African Republic.)
Pierre Kalck. La Documentation française, 1971. 83p. 6 maps. bibliog.
(Notes et Etudes Documentaires no. 3833–34).
This work presents an overall study of Central Africa ten years after its independence.
After a geographical, historical and demographic survey, follow details about the
political and administrative institutions of the time, and studies on economic and
financial development, as well as the cultural and social evolution of the country.

5 **Central African Republic, a failure in de-colonisation.**
Pierre Kalck, translated from the French by Barbara Thomson. London:
Pall Mall, 1971. 206p. map. bibliog. (Pall Mall Library of African
Affairs).
After a general introduction to the country and the people, the author analyses the
four stages of its evolution: the colony of Ubangi-Shari; the emancipation of the
Central African people; the building of a nation; and military leadership. In the last
fifteen pages the author severely criticizes developments and conditions during the first
ten years of independence.

6 **The Central African Republic: the continent's hidden heart.**
Thomas O'Toole. Boulder, Colorado: Westview Press, 1986. 174p.
(Profiles/Nations of Contemporary Africa Series).
Apart from the present author's own *Central African Republic: a failure in de-
colonisation* (q.v.) this is the only major English-language work on the Central African
Republic. It examines the country's tumultuous past and current difficulties, the nature
of the present political situation, and the roots of this situation in the colonial and
precolonial periods. The author also focuses on the roles of ethnicity, emerging urban
problems, class formation, education and religion including the social and cultural
changes that the nation is currently undergoing. Finally, he realistically assesses the
viability of the present government as a vehicle for economic development, stability,
and reform.

7 **L'Oubangui face à l'avenir.** (Ubangi facing the future.)
André Teulières. Paris: Editions de l'Union Française, 1953. 135p.
maps.
At the end of his colonial service in Ubangi, Captain André Teulières, chief of staff for
the former governor, Pierre Delteil, considers the colony's future. Written at a time
when the prospect of independence still seemed to be distant, the book is, however,
well-documented and contains data collected from administrative reports of that
period, as well as many of the author's own observations.

8 **L'Afrique Equatoriale Française.** (French Equatorial Africa.)
Edouard Trezenem. Paris: Editions maritimes et coloniales, 1955. 208p.
A fairly brief presentation of the French colony of French Equatorial Africa, by a
colonial adminstrator who served in the region for thirty years.

9   **Atlas de la République Centrafricaine.** (An atlas of the Central African
    Republic.)
    Edited by Pierre Vennetier.   Paris: Editions Jeune Afrique, 1984. 63p.
    39 maps.

This work is in fact a collection of clear and well-documented articles on various
aspects of the Central African Republic: its land-locked position, relief and geology;
climate; vegetation and fauna; soils; prehistory and history; ethnic groups; population;
villages and towns; agriculture; animal breeding and fishing; wood economy; mines;
industries and cottage industries; communication and transport; education; health;
tourism; and perspectives for development. It forms an essential introduction to any in-
depth study.

10   **L'Afrique Equatoriale Française.** (French Equatorial Africa.)
    Henri Zieglé.   Paris: Berger-Levrault, 1952. 199p.

Director of the information services of FEA, Zieglé has written this comprehensive
book, which for the first time does not hide the gross mistakes made by both the
colonial administrators and private companies – mistakes that have jeopardized the
country's development.

Historical dictionary of the Central African Republic.
See item no. 180.

**Bangui, capitale d'un pays enclavé d'Afrique Centrale. Etude historique et
géographique.** (Bangui, capital of a land-locked country of Central Africa: an
historical and geographical study.)
See item no. 344.

L'Afrique Centrale. (Central Africa.)
See item no. 355.

Réalités oubanguiennes. (Ubangian realities.)
See item no. 393.

Geography and Geology

11 **Géologie du diamant, tome II: Gisements africains.** (The geology of the diamond, volume II: African deposits.)
    G. Bardet. Paris: Mémoires du BRGM no. 83, 1974, 226p.
A collection of monographs concerning the various diamond deposits of Central Africa.

12 **Etude pétrographique et géochimique des profils d'altération latéritique cuirassés dans le sud-est de la République Centrafricaine.** (A petrographical and geochemical study of lateritic weathering profiles capped in oxides of iron in the South-East of the Central African Republic.)
    A. Beauvais. Bangui: Centre ORSTOM, 1989. (Géodynamique 4.2, p. 71–91).
The author presents a geomorphological, genetic and geodynamic analysis of three ferric/ferrous systems.

13 **Géologie de la région de Bria et d'Ippy (République Centrafricaine). Contribution à l'étude de la migmatisation.** (The geology of the region of Bria and Ippy [Central African Republic]: a contribution to the study of migmatization.)
    Bernard Bessoles. Paris: Mémoires du BRGM no. 18, 1962. 205p. map.
The main part of this study is devoted to the early Precambrian period, characterized by the intensity of migmatization. The rest concerns the sandstone of Mouka from the Kwango age, i.e., the Cretaceous period.

14 **Géologie de l'Afrique. Volume II. La chaîne pan-africaine, zone mobile d'Afrique centrale et zone mobile soudanaise.** (The geology of Africa: Volume II; the pan-African chain, the mobile zone of Central Africa and Sudan.)
Bernard Bessoles. Paris: Mémoires du BRGM no. 92, 1980. 398p.

This report concerning several countries of tropical Africa (including the Central African Republic), focuses on the pre-Cambrian formations, the young granites after the pan-African cycle, as well as the nature of the contact between the mobile zone and the cratons of the West of Central Africa and the Congo.

15 **Le bassin du fleuve Chari, monographie hydrologique.** (The Shari River basin, a hydrological monograph.)
R. Billon, J. Guiscafre, J. Herbaud, G. Oberlin. Paris: ORSTOM, 1974. 450p. 5 maps.

The Shari basin is shaped like a large fan, covering about one-third of the area of the Central African Republic. The name Shari, however, was only given to the Chadian part of the river in Bagirmi.

16 **Note sur la découverte scientifique de la Centrafrique. Une erreur à corriger: le cours amont du Chari n'est ni le Bamingui, ni l'Aouk, mais l'Ouham-Bahr-Sara.** (A comment on the scientific discovery of Central Africa. An error to be corrected: the true upper course of the Shari is neither the Bamingui nor the Aouk, but the Ouham-Bahr-Sara.)
Yves Boulvert. Bondy, France: MRP, ORSTOM, November 1982. 11p.

The French explorer, Emile Gentil, had succeeded in establishing the idea that the Bamingui represented the upper course of the Shari. All the hydrological measurements show, however, that the true Shari is the Ouham-Bahr-Sara, as the explorers Casimir Maistre and Commander Lenfant had asserted.

17 **Note sur la découverte scientifique de la Centrafrique. Une erreur à corriger: le massif des Bongo 1400m.** (A comment on the scientific discovery of Central Africa. An error to be corrected: the Bongo massif 1400m.)
Yves Boulvert. Bondy, France: MRP, ORSTOM, November 1982. 3p. 2 maps.

Geographical maps mention a mountain range in the northeast of the Central African Republic that exceeds 1,000 metres and that since 1912 has been called the Bongo massif, from the name of a population that no longer exists. Boulvert shows, however, that it is only the escarpment of a sandstone plateau reaching a height of 950 metres.

18 **Note morphologique sur l'interfluve Congo-Nil.** (A morphological comment on the Congo-Nile interfluve.)
Yves Boulvert. Bondy, France: MRP, ORSTOM, December 1982. 9p.

Boulvert shows that the Congo-Nile interfluve in the east of the Central African Republic does not correspond in any way to a mountain range, but to a simple hardened cornice. The dividing line of the waterways was adopted in 1899 as the border between the Anglo-Egyptian Sudan and the French Upper Ubangi. It remains the present-day border between the Central African Republic and the Sudan. The region has no inhabitants. In the past, it formed a caravan route linking the north of Africa to the centre of the continent.

19 **Aplanissements en Afrique centrale. Relations avec le cuirassement, la technique, le bioclimat. Problèmes posès, progrès des connaissances.** (The levelling process in Central Africa: its connection with hardening, technics and the bio-climate; problems and the present state of knowledge.)
Yves Boulvert. *Bulletin de l'Association Géographique française*, vol. 4 (1985), p. 300–309. map.

In the heart of the African continent, the Central African Republic offers a sequence of planation levels and eroded slopes. The same iron crust fossilizes all these levels. However, the Central African surface is scattered with old remnant buttes. Recent progress in geology supports the tectonic explanation of this sequence of levels. In spite of small differences in height, scarps have an important influence on climatic, vegetal and pedological differentiations.

20 **Contribution à l'étude du milieu naturel centrafricain. Exploitation et corrélation des données obtenues par photo-interpretation, télédétection et travaux de terrain pour la réalisation des cartes pédologiques, phyto-géographiques et géomorphologiques à 1/1,000,000 de la République Centrafricaine.** (A contribution to the study of the natural environment of Central Africa. The exploitation and correlation of data obtained by photo-interpretation, teledetection and fieldwork in order to produce pedological, phyto-geographical and geomorphological maps of 1:1,000,000 of the Central African Republic.)
Yves Boulvert. Bangui; Dijon, France: Centre ORSTOM et Centre des Sciences de la terre, Université de Bourgogne, doctorat d'Etat en sciences naturelles thesis, 27 June 1990.

In order to draw a pedological map, an area of the Central African Republic has been studied by detailed photo-interpretation. Many descriptions of pedestrian itineraries across the land, with pedological profiles, particularly along toposequences are also given. This local study had been supplemented by accounts of relief and types of vegetation and it has gradually become an integrated survey of the natural environment.

21 **Evolution de la granulométrie et du classement des sables de l'Oubangui depuis la confluence du M'Bomou et de l'Ouellé jusqu'à la frontière centrafricano-congolaise.** (The evolution of granulometry and the classification of sands of the Ubangi from the confluence of the M'Bomu and the Uele to the Central Africano-Congolese border.)
Claude Censier. Bangui; Dijon, France: Université de Bangui and Centre des Sciences de la terre, Université de Bourgogne, 1990. 11p.

This granulometric approach carried out on sand samples taken from the whole length of the Ubangi makes it possible to determine the zones of the Ubangi basin subjected to erosion.

22 **Dynamique sédimentaire d'un système fluviatile diamantifère mézosoïque. La formation de Carnot (République Centrafricaine).** (Sedimentary dynamics of a Mezozoic diamond-yielding river system. The Carnot formation [Central African Republic].)
Claude Censier. MA thesis, Université de Bourgogne, Dijon, France, 1989. 591p.

The first part of this thesis is a presentation of basement formations and Mambéré Glacial Formation, on which rests the Carnot Formation, in order to specify the geological history and the pre-Mezozoïc paleogeographical framework of the western Central African Republic. Secondly there is a detailed geological study of the Carnot formation. The third section considers the geology of diamonds in the western part of the country. The various types of diamantiferous deposits are described in their geological context and the origin of diamonds is studied in the alluvial context.

23 **Aperçu sur le climat centrafricain.** (A survey of the Central African climate.)
A. Chabra. Bangui: ASECNA, 1962. 25p.

In central Africa, the humid tropical climate in the south becomes progressively drier as one moves north. The author describes here the three large climatic zones of the country.

24 **Note préliminaire sur l'hydrologie de la région de Bangui.** (A preliminary comment on the hydrology of the Bangui region.)
Maurice Cornacchia, Loïc Giorgi, Jean-Claude Lachaud. Montpellier, France: 110e Congrès national des societés savantes, 1985, Faculté des Sciences, fascicle VI, p. 331–42.

For a long time the nature of the substratum of the Bangui plain was unknown, hidden under huge deposits of fluvio-lakeside formations. In 1972, surveys revealed a karst massif of considerable length and thickness. A second water layer, fed by the river and protected from any outside attacks, and constituting a huge reservoir was also revealed.

Geography and Geology

25 **L'Afrique centrale et orientale.** (Central and eastern Africa.)
J. Denis, Pierre Vennetier, J. Wilmet. Paris: Presses Universitaires de
France, 1971. 295p. (Collection Magellan).
The geography of a land-locked country like the Central African Republic cannot be
studied independently from that of the neighbouring countries. This work, therefore,
places the Central African Republic within the context of central and eastern Africa as
a whole.

26 **La République Centrafricaine. Géographie.** (The Central African
Republic: a geography.)
Nadine Donnet, Jean-François Le Borgne, Jean-Louis Piermay. Paris:
Hatier, 1975. 79p. (Collection André Journaux).
Basically a handbook for Central African schoolchildren.

27 **Seismological investigation of the Bangui magnetic anomaly region and its
relations to the margin of the Congo craton.**
Catherine Dorbath, Louis Dorbath, Roland Gaulon, Denis
Hatzfeld. *Earth and Planetary Science Letters* no. 75 (1985), p. 231–44.
Considers the Bangui magnetic anomaly region and seismic velocity distribution and
asserts that the abnormal magnetic field could be due to a deep structure with a higher
susceptibility. This Bangui anomaly is of particular interest because it is an unusually
large, isolated anomaly occurring over a stable continental interior.

28 **Agroclimatologie du Centrafrique.** (Agroclimatology of Central Africa.)
Pierre Franquin, Roland Diziain, Jean-Paul Cointepas, Yves
Boulvert. Paris: ORSTOM, 1988. 522p. 33 maps. bibliog. (Collection
Initiations-Documentations Techniques no. 71).
This study considers the three types of climate existing in central Africa (Guinean
forest climate, Sudano-Guinean climate and Sahelo-Sudanese climate), the conditions
which create these climates and the characteristics of their seasons. The quantitative
data on the agronomical character comes from ninety-five stations set up in the
country. Four processes of pedo-genesis appear: ferrallitization, ferruginization,
vertisolization, and hydromorphy. Agricultural land represents only one per cent of the
territory. The authors state that the water reserves of central Africa are large and have
previously been under-estimated.

29 **Données nouvelles sur la géologie de la région de Bangui.** (New data
about the geology of the Bangui region.)
Loïc Giorgi, Maurice Cornacchia. *Annales du Musée Royal d'Afrique
Centrale* [Tervuren, Belgium] *Série Sciences-Géologie no. 93*, (1986),
p. 1–33.
The Bangui region is characterized by very complex tectonics with a network of
inversed faults. Although the presence of hard quartzite has presented an interest for
construction, the mediocre soils, often transformed into hard layers, pose a problem.

30   **Le modelé des grès, problèmes généraux.** (Sandstone relief, general
problems.)
Monique Mainguet.   Paris: Institut Géographique National, 1972. 657p.

Describes how the central African shield is covered in intercalory continental
sandstone deposits, often referred to as Carnot sandstone in the west and Mouka
sandstone in the east.

31   **Géologie et ressources minérales de la République Centrafricaine.** (The
geology and mineral resources of the Central African Republic.)
Jean-Louis Mestraud, Bernard Bessoles.   Orléans, France: Mémoires du
BRGM, 1982. 185p. bibliog.

This work reveals the main geological features of the Central African Republic, and is
based on fifteen years of surveys carried out by these two geologists. It is an essential
aid for all those who are working on the geology and mineral resources of the country.
The volume contains an exhaustive bibliography of publications which appeared prior
to 1963.

32   **Bilan annuel et variations saisonnières des flux particulaires du Congo à
Brazzaville et de l'Oubangui à Bangui.** (The suspended load of the
Congo and Ubangi rivers.)
Jean-Claude Olivry, Jean-Pierre Bricquet, Jean-Pierre
Thiebaux.   Montpellier, France: ORSTOM. 1989. 124p.

Presents the results of a large scientific programme in the Congo basin which examined
the fluctuation of suspended and dissolved fluxes and compared the characteristics of
mechanical and biogeochemical erosion with hydroclimatological regions in equatorial
ecosystems. Measurements were made on the Congo at Brazzaville and on the Ubangi
at Bangui.

33   **Les sols de la République Centrafricaine.** (The soils of the Central
African Republic.)
Paul Quantin.   Paris: ORSTOM, 1964. 114p. (Mémoires de
l'ORSTOM, no. 16).

Quantin makes a preliminary assessment of soil distribution and examines its relationship to the climate and substratum.

34   **Les ceintures de roches vertes de la République Centrafricaine. (Bandas,
Boufoyo, Bogoin, Mbomou). Contribution à la connaissance du
précambrien du nord du craton du Congo.** (The belts of green rocks of
the Central African Republic [Bandas, Boufoyo, Bogoin, Mbomu]. A
contribution to the knowledge of the Precambrian period in the north of
the Congo craton.)
Jean-Louis Poidevin.   Doctorat ès sciences thesis, Université Blaise
Pascal, à Clermont-Ferrand, France, 1991. 458p.

Although the northern part of the central African shield belongs to the mobile zone
(superior Precambrian), the extreme south of the country, according to the author,
joins the Congolese craton.

35 **The Bangui magnetic anomaly: its geological origin.**
Robert D. Regan, Bruce D. Marsh. *Journal of Geophysical Research*,
vol. 87, no. 32 (1982), p. 1107-20.

This analysis, the first of its type, is not complete. However, by considering the
satellite data, a plausible geological origin can be put forward to explain the anomaly.

36 **Géographie-Empire Centrafricain.** (A geography. Central African
Empire.)
Pierre Sammy. Paris: Hatier, 1977. 76p.

A school-book aimed at pupils in the intermediate classes in primary schools in central
Africa.

La République Centrafricaine. (The Central African Republic.)
See item no. 2.

Atlas de la République Centrafricaine. (Atlas of the Central African
Republic.)
See item no. 9.

Maps

37 **Carte-guide de Bangui au 1:20,000.** (Map-guide of Bangui drawn to a scale of 1:20,000.)
Institut Géographique National. Paris: The Institute, 1991.
This is the first map of Bangui to appear since 1970. During the intervening period the population of the city has increased by some 144,000. The map covers an area of 400 square kilometres and incorporates the area within the Bangui communal boundaries and the potential extension zones to the west of the city.

38 **Carte de la République Centrafricaine au 1:200,000.** (Map of the Central African Republic drawn to a scale of 1:200,000.)
Institut Géographique National. Paris: The Institute, 1960-84.
The Central African Republic territory is covered by sixty-three pages of maps drawn and revised by French geographers between 1960 and 1984. These maps correspond to squares of 1° latitude and 1° longitude, forming an excellent guide. Unfortunately, in 1991, thirty-six of these maps were out of print.

39 **Carte générale de la République Centrafricaine au 1:1,500,000.** (A general map of the Central African Republic drawn to a scale of 1:1,500,000.)
Institut Géographique National. Paris: The Institute, 1980.
The 1980 edition of this road map, consists of a useful list of place names and is particularly suitable for tourists.

40 **Carte internationale du monde au 1:1,000,000 surcharge OACI.** (International world map drawn to a scale of 1:1,000,000 produced under the auspices of the Organisation Internationale de l'Aviation Civile.)
Institut Géographique National. Paris: The Institute, 1963, 1965.
The following pages cover Central African Republic territory: NA Ouesso, NB Bangui, NB Bangassou and NC Am Timan.

Maps

41 **International map of the world 1:2,000,000.**
Defense Mapping Agency. Washington, DC: The Agency. 1969-1977.
In the Africa section, the following sheets are of interest: 19 (Bangui edition 6 DMATC), 18 (Douala edition 6 DMATC), 23 (Kisangani edition 5 AMS) and 22 (Libreville edition 5 AMS).

42 **Carte géologique de la République Centrafricaine au 1:1,500,000.**
(Geological map of the Central African Republic drawn to a scale of 1:1,500,000.)
Drawn by Jean-Louis Mestraud. Paris: BRGM, 1963.
This new geological map takes into account the important work done by the French 'Commissariat à l'énergie atomique' around the uranium-bearing basin of Bakouma, as well as research carried out by French geologists. It questions the time-span which has previously been accepted as the Precambrian era.

43 **Carte pédologique de la République Centrafricaine 1:1,000,000.**
(Pedological map of the Central African Republic: explanatory leaflet no. 100.)
Yves Boulvert. Paris: ORSTOM, 1983. 2 sheets (west and east). 126p.
The old pedological sketches on the scale: 1:5,000,000 gave only a rough idea of soil distribution in Central Africa according to climate and substratum. This new 1:1,000,000 pedological map is the synthesis of thirty years of research carried out by ORSTOM. It tries to represent the soils according to the relief.

44 **Carte phytogéographique de la République Centrafricaine à 1:1,000,000.**
Notice explicative no. 104. (A phytogeographical map of the Central African Republic drawn to a scale of 1:1,000,000: explanatory note no. 104.)
Yves Boulvert. Paris: ORSTOM, 1986. 3 sheets. 131p.
Until now there has only been simple phytogeographical sketches of Central Africa drawn to a scale of 1:5,000,000, dividing the country into four regions according to the parallels and the meridians. This map, compiled by Yves Boulvert, uses the inventories drawn up by agronomists and foresters. It also provides the first phytogeographical interpretation established from aerial cover, e.g. Landsat pictures. This map has enabled the surface area covered by dense forest to be increased from 40,000 to 50,000 square kilometres, including the forests of Ouham, Kemo, Upper-Kotto and Upper-Mbomou.

45 **Carte oro-hydrographique de la République Centrafricaine à 1:1,000,000.**
Notice explicative no. 106. (Oro-hydrological map of the Central African Republic drawn to a scale of 1:1,000,000: explanatory note no. 106.)
Yves Boulvert. Paris: ORSTOM, 1987. 2 sheets. 118p.
This map depicts a country of average altitude, fed by numerous water courses forming an easily accessible platform between the basins of the Congo, the Chad, the Niger and the Nile. Less than two per cent of the area is at an altitude of more than 1000 metres. Half of the country is situated between 400 and 600 metres and two-thirds of the country belongs to the Congo Basin, whereas one-third belongs to the Chad basin.

46   **Carte pédologique de Bangui à 1:200,000. Notice explicative no. 64.**
      (Pedological map of Bangui drawn to a scale of 1:200,000: explanatory
      leaflet no. 64.)
      Yves Boulvert.   Bondy, France: ORSTOM, 1976. 116p.

This map is the synthesis of thirty years of research carried out by ORSTOM. The
percentage of cultivated land is estimated at one per cent and at any one time a similar
percentage lies fallow. Boulvert believes, however, that a third of the Central African
territory could be used for cultivation. A geomorphological map by the same author
(drawn to a scale of 1:1,000,000) is being prepared by ORSTOM.

47   **Inventaire cartographique de la République Centrafricaine.**
      (Cartographic inventory of the Central African Republic.)
      Jean Cantournet.   Paris: Societé d'ethnographie, 1987. 183p. (Université
      de Paris X, Recherches Oubanguiennes no. 9.)

The author has drawn up a list of all the surveys, sketches, plans or maps devoted to
the Central African Republic that exist today. It only focuses on the documentary
collection kept in France, however, and is therefore not exhaustive. Certain regions
described in these documents are now deserted and access is difficult, but many of
these sketches and old maps remain the only historical evidence of human settlements
which have now disappeared. By contrast, modern maps sometimes display a
considerable lack of information, notably in the orographic and hydrographic fields.
This inventory consists of 817 references, plus a classification according to scale, a
chronological list year by year, thematic lists and an index of authors.

Atlas de la République Centrafricaine. (Atlas of the Central African
Republic.)
See item no. 9.

Tourist Guides

48 **Afrique Equatoriale Française.** (French Equatorial Africa.)
Robert Delavignette, with geographical, ethnological and economic
notes by Jacques Vulaines. Paris: Les albums des Guides Bleus,
Hachette, 1957. 127p.

Delavignette, the honorary Governor-General of the time, praises the original concept
which led to the unification of the huge area of land stretching from Gabon to Chad
under the French flag. The 'Federation of French Equatorial Africa' was the
realization of the explorer Paul Crampel's dream. A selection of beautiful illustrations
with comments by Jacques Vulaines completes the work.

49 **Guide. Chasse et tourisme en République Centrafricaine.** (Guide.
Hunting and tourism in the Central African Republic.)
Marcel Diki-Kidiri, Jean-Pierre Schenardi. Paris: Editions de la
Pommeraye, 1982. 141p.

A work providing some comments on the country as a whole as well as the main
species of animals. There is some practical advice for the tourist and notably the
hunter. Common phrases in the Sango language are explained.

50 **Centrafrique, Congo, Gabon.** (Central Africa, Congo, Gabon.)
Arlette Eyraud. Paris: Hatier et Air Afrique, 1979. 144p. maps.

This work contains good articles by various specialists on the geography, the history,
the ethnography, the political organization and the economic life of each of these three
states. Numerous itineraries, with maps, sketches and photographs are included.
Practical information for the traveller is also provided. In 1980, this guide won the
'Boussole d'or' (The golden compass), the prize for the best French tourist guide.

51 **Oubangui-Chari, paradis du tourisme cynégétique.** (Ubangi-Shari, paradise of cynegetic tourism.)
René Gauze.   Caen: Imprimerie Ozanne, 1958. 381p. 9 maps.

The author was Bangui's police superintendent in the 1950s and he has written the first tourist guide devoted solely to the territory of Ubangi-Shari. It offers the tourist a series of routes with comments on the colonial history of the regions passed through.

52 **Afrique Centrale: les Républiques d'expression française.** (Central Africa: the French-speaking Republics.)
Gilbert Houlet.   Paris: Les Guides bleus, Hachette, 1962. 533p.

Houlet has drawn together much useful information particularly for those wishing to visit the city of Bangui and the surrounding area. This guide was written by the author after a journey lasting no less than two years.

Expeditions and Exploration

53 A la conquête du Tchad. (The conquest of Chad.)
Harry Alis. Paris: Hachette, 1891. 296p.

The journalist, Hippolyte Percher, who wrote this book under the pseudonym of Harry Alis, was the instigator of the Crampel expedition. He was responsible for the foundation of the 'Comité de l'Afrique française' on 18 November 1890, and inspired many great French explorers to journey to Africa. In June 1890, this book was used to plan the French missions to the Lake Chad region.

54 Nos Africains. (Our Africans.)
Harry Alis. Paris: Hachette, 1894. 568p.

This book is the continuation of Alis's earlier work (see item 53) about the French expeditions in Central Africa. The author reviews the explorations organized under the aegis of the 'Comité de l'Afrique française' from 1890 to 1894, and advocates the creation of large concessionary companies to exploit the territory that had become French.

55 Carnets du Congo. Voyage avec Gide. (Notes of the Congo: a journey with Gide.)
Marc Allegret. Paris: Presses du CNRS, collection Singulier-pluriel, 1987. 295p.

Marc Allegret, who accompanied André Gide in 1925, brought back a film of the journey, numerous photographs and he also kept a diary. This diary was not published until 1987 with annotations by Daniel Durosay. Its interest lies in its unusual perspective on the life and people of the region.

56 **Reisen und Entdeckungen in Nord und Central Afrika in den Jahren 1849 bis 1855.** (Journeys and discoveries in north and central Africa from 1849 until 1855.)
Heinrich Barth. Gotha, Germany: J. Perthes, 1857. 5 vols. English edition, London: Longman, Brown, 1857. 5 vols. French edition, Paris: Firmin-Didot, 1859-61. 4 vols.

In this volume Barth, a German explorer, recounts how he met a faki named Sambo. The faki held an important place in Muslim Central Afirca as the secretaries of the kings and chiefs because unlike their superiors they were literate. Sambo, a Bagirmian, impressed Barth because he recited entire passages from Plato in Arabic. He told Barth that a large pro-slavery expedition had, in 1824, reached a sizeable river in the south flowing towards the west (the Ubangi).

57 **Rapport sur le haut Oubangui, le Mbomou et le Bahr el Ghazal.** (Report on upper Ubangi, Mbomu and Bahr al-Ghazal.)
Albert Bonnel de Mézières. Paris: Imprimerie Albouy, 1901. 209p.

In order to examine the problems of exploitation caused by the Belgian evacuation of the Bandia and Zande sultanates, the private French company called 'Syndicat du Tchad et de l'Oubangui', authorized Mézières, a former member of the Maistre expedition, to carry out a study.

58 **Haut Oubangui. Exploration de la Kotto.** (Upper Ubangi: the exploration of the Kotto.)
Lieutenant Bos. *Revue Coloniale* (1901-02), p. 319-51.

Lieutenant Bos, a French resident at Bangassou, describes a journey across a region where the inhabitants were terrorized by raids carried out by Muhammad as-Sanusi in order to procure slaves.

59 **Découverte géographique et scientifique de l'Ouest de la Centrafrique.** (The geographical and scientific discovery of West Central Africa.)
Yves Boulvert. Bondy, Paris: MRP, ORSTOM, 1984. 36p.

Boulvert's work covers: the discovery of the Sangha basin (1886-1907); the Wam-Shari problem concerning the true course of the two rivers (1892-1907); the Sangha-Ubangi interfluve; the belatedly explored northwest plateaux of central Africa; and the discovery of the sandstone unity of Gadzi-Carnot. The slow exploration of these regions by the French is noted by the author, as is the fact that the survey of the large waterways was barely finished when these regions were transferred to Germany under a treaty between the two nations signed on 4 November 1911.

60 **Explorateurs méconnus de l'Est Centrafricain.** (Unrecognized explorers
   of East Central Africa.)
   Yves Boulvert. Bondy, France: MRP, ORSTOM, 1984. 36p.
This book consists of two very interesting notes. The first focuses on travellers'
accounts and expeditions in east central Africa before 1885. The second retraces the
history of the Belgian penetration north of Mbomu and east of Kotto between 1891
and 1894. The geographical and historical interest of this region, once well-populated
and an important communications crossroads between the north and the centre of the
continent, but now devoid of humans, is considerable. The author points out that even
the names of the places have disappeared, something that is, according to him,
extremely rare.

61 **Le problème de l'Oubangui-Ouellé ou comment fut exploré et reconstitué
   un réseau hydrographique à la fin du XIX siècle.** (The Ubangi-Uele: the
   exploration and reconstruction of a river system at the end of the 19th
   century.)
   Yves Boulvert. *Sciences Humaines*, vol. 21, no. 4 (1985), p. 389.
   7 maps. bibliog.
Although the course of the Congo was rapidly discovered by Stanley in 1877, it took
twenty years from 1870 to 1890 to explore and understand the Ubangi-Uele river
system in a region which formed the last blank space on the map of Africa. The
geographical reality appeared slowly because of the difficulties faced by the explorers
who were alone in hostile countries and because of politial rivalries over African
partition.

62 **Le Centre de l'Afrique. Autour du Tchad.** (The centre of Africa: around
   Chad.)
   Paul Brunache. Paris: F. Alcan, 1894. 340p. map.
The author, an assistant to the French explorer, Jean Dybowski, recounts his
experiences.

63 **André Gide et l'Afrique. Le rôle de l'Afrique dans la vie et l'oeuvre de
   l'écrivain.** (Andre Gide and Africa: the influence of Africa on the
   writer's life and work.)
   Jacqueline M. Chadourne. Paris: A.G. Nizet, 1968. 213p. 2nd part:
   Afrique noire (Black Africa) p. 132–206.
Gide was only twenty years old when he first dreamed of making his famous journey to
equatorial Africa. He undertook this venture in the mid-1920s (when he was in his late
50s) when the minister of the colonies vested him with an official mission. He was
inspired by Joseph Conrad's *Heart of Darkness*.

64 **Mission Chari-Lac Tchad 1902-1904. L'Afrique Centrale Française –
   Récit de la mission.** (The Shari-Lake Chad mission 1902-1904: French
   central Africa; an account of the mission.)
   Auguste Chevalier. Paris: A. Challamel, 1908. 776p. maps.
Professor Chevalier, a distinguished botanist, was put in charge of the first French
scientific mission in Upper-Shari.

65 **Voyage de M.F.J. Clozel.** (M.F.J. Clozel's journey.)
Marie-François Joseph Clozel. *Bulletin de la Société de Géographie de l'Est*, vol. 18 (1987), p. 28-104.

In September 1893, the 'Comité de l'Afrique française' decided to organize a new expedition under Clozel with the aim of reaching Chad by the Sangha. Clozel changed his mind about proceeding in July 1894 at Berberati, when he learned of the clauses of the Franco-German agreement of 15 March 1894, which altered the boundaries of French and German territories in the area. Clozel now recommended a military operation against Rabah, who had just conquered Bagirmi.

66 **Deux ans chez les anthropophages et les sultans du Centre-Africain.** (Two years with the anthropophagites and sultans of the Centre of Africa.)
Raymond Colrat de Montrosier. Paris: Plon, 1902. 326p. map.

The author was a member of the second Bonnel de Mézières expedition of 1898, charged with carrying out a commercial suvey of Upper Ubangi. He considered the building of several railway lines to be essential, and recommended the withdrawal of the Bandia and Zande sultans' authority.

67 **Du Congo au lac Tchad. La brousse telle qu'elle est, les gens tels qu'ils sont.** (From the Congo to Lake Chad: the real bush, the real people.)
Docteur J. Decorse. Paris: Asselin et Houzeau, 1906. 347p.

The author accompanied Professor Chevalier on his mission in Upper-Shari (1902-04) and here records observations about the Sara people, who were at that time being pursued by Muhammad as-Sanusi who was attempting to procure slaves.

68 **La route du Tchad. De Loango au Chari.** (The road to Chad. From Loango to Shari.)
Jean Dybowski. Paris: Firmin-Didot, 1893. 381p. map.

Jean Dybowski, the professor of agriculture at the school of Grignon, was appointed by the 'Comité de l'Afrique française' at the end of 1890, to reinforce the Crampel expedition and create a base in the Shari basin. He also concluded treaties with the Banda chiefs. The book includes 136 drawings.

69 **Voyage au Ouadây.** (A journey to Wadaï.)
Cheykh Mohammed ibn Omar el Tounsy, translated into French by Docteur Perron. Paris: Duprat, 1851. 756p. map.

An interesting description of the kingdom of Wadaï at the beginning of the nineteenth century by this well-informed Tunisian. He points out that this State extends to the south of Bahr Salamat through the Dar el Djénakhéra (Sara), the Dar Sila and the Dar Rawna (Rounga) regions. He indicates three main rivers flowing to the west.

Expeditions and Exploration

70 **Voyage au Dârfour.** (A journey to Darfur.)
Cheykh Mohammed ibn Omar el Tounsy, translated into French by
Docteur Perron. Paris: Duprat, 1845. 480p. map.

This extremely useful document about the kingdom of Darfur at the beginning of the
nineteenth century contains numerous notes on the Dar Fertit, i.e. the northeastern
regions of the present-day Central African Republic, which was the slave-hunting
territory for the Forians. The author describes the region of Dar Schala (Dar Chala),
the Dar Bâya (Kreich country) and Dar Benda (Banda country). According to Perron,
a slave-hunting operation had reached the Mbomu and the Ubangi after a five-month
campaign (p. 274 onwards).

71 **Au vieux Congo – Notes de route (1884-1891).** (The old Congo: travel
notes 1844-1891.)
Alfred Fourneau. Paris: Editions du Comité de l'Afrique française,
1932. 324p.

At the beginning of 1891, Pierre Savorgnan de Brazza had decided to send two
expeditions to the Upper Sangha. The party commanded by Alfred Fourneau was
attacked by the Gbaya in May 1891 and had to withdraw, even though four
protectorate treaties had been concluded with different chiefs.

72 **Voyage au Congo, suivi du retour du Tchad.** (A journey to the Congo,
followed by the return from Chad.)
André Gide. Paris: Gallimard, 1927-28. New edition, Paris: Gallimard,
1981. Collection Idées 493p. English edition, New York: Alfred Knopf,
1981. New German edition, Stuttgart, Germany: Deutsche
Verlaganstalt, 1992.

The travel diaries of the famous novelist revealed colonial atrocities perpetrated in
Lobaye and in Upper Sangha. They shook French opinion at a time when everything
was being done to cover up the negative effects of the colonial régime in the eyes of
the public. In 1927, this work was distributed in Geneva to members of the BIT
(Bureau International du Travail) now called the OIT (Organisation Internationale du
Travail) as a document about forced labour in the colonies.

73 **Exploration of the tributaries of the Congo between Leopoldville and
Stanley Falls.** George Grenfell. *Proceedings of the Royal Geographical
Society*, vol. 8, no. 10, (1886), p. 627-33.

Accompanied by the American doctor Sims, the English pastor George Grenfell was
the first European to reach the present-day site of Bangui, in February 1885. The
steam-boat *Peace*, on which they travelled, was obliged to make an about-turn owing
to the hostility of the river-side populations.

74 **Mission de délimitation de l'AEF et du Soudan Anglo-Egyptien.** (An expedition to mark the boundaries of French Equatorial Africa and Anglo-Egyptian Sudan.) Lieutenant-Colonel Grossard. Paris: Librairie Larose, 1925. 343p. 10 maps.

Between 1922 and 1924, an Anglo-French expedition (led by Grossard and Pearson) literally defined the border (by placing posts in the ground) between French Equatorial Africa and Sudan (from Libya to Zaïre), and carried out a remarkable topographical study, which provided a great deal of valuable information about the regions visited.

75 **La croisière noire. Expédition Citroën – Centre-Afrique.** (The crossing of Black Africa: the Citroën-Central Africa Expedition.) Georges Marie Haardt, Louis Audoin-Dubreuil. Paris: Plon, 1927. 317p. 2 maps.

On 28 October 1924, the Citroën-Central Africa expedition which crossed Africa departed from Algeria. The convoy of cars reached Chad on 24 December, then Bangui on 11 January 1925. After travelling round the distant regions of Yalinga and Birao, the cars headed towards the Belgian Congo and eastern Africa. Numerous observations about the regions covered are included here.

76 **Mission du capitaine Jacquier dans l'arrière-pays des sultanats du haut-Oubangui et sur la frontière du Soudan Anglo-Égyptien (1 octobre 1910-21 février 1911).** (Captain Jacquier's mission to the hinterland of the sultanates of Upper-Ubangi and along the Anglo-Egyptian Sudan border (1 October 1910-21 February 1911.) Capitaine Jules Jacquier. Versailles, France: Service historique des troupes de marine, France, 1912. 166p. map.

The author, a French officer in charge of the region of Mobayé, undertook the reconnaissance of the regions between Dar al-Kuti and the Bandia and Zande sultanates in 1911. They had been abandoned since their evacuation by the Belgians in 1894. This document is of vital importance to Central African history.

77 **Reisen in Afrika 1875-1886.** (Travels in Africa during the years 1875-1886.) Edited by Wilhelm Junker from his diaries in collaboration with R. Buchta. Vienna and Olmütz [now called Olomouc]: E. Hölzel, 1889-91. 3 vols. Translated into English by A.H. Keane. London: Chapman & Hall, 1890. 3 vols.

Eric de Dampierre called this German explorer's work 'a classic and a monument of precision'. Coming from the Nile like the explorer, Schweinfurth, Junker reached the Mbomu and the Uele, the upper course of the Ubangi, and noted that these rivers flowed towards the west. This work is essential for an understanding of the history of central Africa and especially that of the east of the present-day Central African Republic. Apart from some pages translated into French by A. de Haulleville in the Brussels *Congo illustré* (1891-92), Junker's work has never been translated into French. It remains unknown to the central Africans.

78 **La découverte des grandes sources du centre de l'Afrique. Rivières de vie, rivières de mort. Nana, Ouam, Pendé.** (The discovery of the major river sources in central Africa: rivers of life, rivers of death; Nana, Ouam, Pendé.)
Commandant Lenfant. Paris: Hachette, 1909. 284p. map.

This expedition organized by the French in the west of Central Africa, aimed to establish a new communications link with Chad. The writer, Ernest Psichari, was a member of this mission.

79 **Lupton Bey and the Bahr el Ghazal.**
Frank Lupton. *Proceedings of the Royal Geographical Society*, vol. 5, no. 7 (1883), p. 350-81 and 482-83; vol. 6, no. 5 (1884), p. 152–53 and p. 246-55. map.

Lupton was appointed governor of Bahr al-Ghazal by Gordon Pacha in 1881, and carried out a remarkable raid in the east of the present-day central African territory as far as Kotto, in 1882. The areas he crossed were well-populated and prosperous.

80 **A travers l'Afrique Centrale. Du Congo au Niger.** (Crossing central Africa: from the Congo to the Niger.)
Casimir Maistre. Paris: Hachette, 1895. 302p.

Formed at the beginning of 1892, the Maistre expedition was sent out to reinforce the Dybowski mission. Setting off from the base at Kemo which had been established by Dybowski, Maistre crossed the Manja and Sara regions, and concluded treaties and journeyed back to the Atlantic coast via the Bénué and the Niger.

81 **From the Congo to the Niger and the Nile.**
Herzog A.F. zu Mecklenburg. London; Leipzig: Brickhauss, 1913. 2 vols.

The German expedition described here was led by a member of the royal family of Prussia and carried out some studies, notably botanical, in the region of the Ubangi. It was seen by the French as the forerunner to German expansion in the area.

82 **Sahara and Sudan. IV Wadaï and Darfur.**
Gustav Nachtigal, translated from the German by Allan G.B. Fisher, Humphrey J. Fisher. London: Christopher Hurst, 1971. 439p.

This work was translated from Nachtigal's *Sahara und Sudan, Ergebnisse von Reisen in Afrika IV*. After having explored the regions of the Shari and the Logone, the famous German explorer reached the Wadaï in 1873. He planned a journey to the south of Bahr Salamat but he gave up because he was infected with malaria. A Bornuan, Ali Fentami, had given him a lot of information about the areas belonging to the current Central African Republic and had even taught him elements of the Banda language. The notes taken by Nachtigal during his stay in Wadaï have also been translated into French by Joost van Vollenhoven in nos 3-10 of *Bulletin du Comité de l'Afrique Française, Renseignements Coloniaux*, (1903).

83   **La mission Crampel.** (The Crampel expedition.)
     Albert Nebout. *Le Tour du Monde*, vol. 64 (1892), p. 1-65.

After Paul Crampel and Biscarrat were massacred by Muhammad as-Sanusi in April-
May 1891, Albert Nebout made the decision to withdraw with the surviving members
of the expedition. This article attempts above all to justify this retreat.

84   **Rapport général de la mission de délimitation AEF-Cameroun 1912-1913.**
     (A general report about the expedition to mark the boundaries of
     French Equatorial Africa-Cameroon 1912-13.)
     L. Périquet. Paris: Imbans et Chapelot, 1915-16. 3 vols.

Following the transfer of the Sangha river basin and control over the access to the
Ubangi by the Lobaye, from France to Germany in November 1911, the Périquet
expedition was asked to define the new frontier. This enabled Crampel to explore the
unknown basins of the Mbi-Pama. The book contains an interesting study of the flora
and fauna of this region.

85   **The Heart of Africa.**
     Translated into English by E.E. Frewer from Georg Schweinfurth's *Im
     Herzen von Afrika, Reisen und Entdeckungen in Centralen Aequatorial
     Afrika während der Jahre 1868 bis 1871*, Leipzig, Germany, and
     translated into French by H. Loreau, *Voyages et découvertes dans les
     régions inexplorées de l'Afrique Centrale.* Paris: Hachette, 1875. 2 vols.
     508p. and 404p.

Georg Schweinfurth, from Riga, was the first European explorer to recognize the
Congo-Nile interfluve, and to reach the Uele river, near to which he rediscovered the
Akkas pygmies, forgotten since the fifth-century B.C. account by Herodotus.
Schweinfurth also gathered information about the Banda people.

86   **Lettres de l'Ubangi.** (Letters from Ubangi.)
     Lieutenant Stroobant. *Le Mouvement Géographique Brussels*, no. 14
     (5 April 1896) to no. 27 (5 July 1896), 176-341.

Between 1893 and 1894 this Belgian officer explored the region between the Mbomu
and the Kotto rivers, where he founded several colonial administrative posts in the
Congo Free State (which became the Belgian Congo in 1908). Stroobant died on the
return journey and these letters were published posthumously.

87   **L'exploration de l'Oubangui-Doua-Kouyou.** (The exploration of the
     Ubangi-Doua-Kouyou.)
     Capitaine Alphonse Vangèle. *Bulletin de la Société Royale Belge de
     Géographie* (Brussels), vol. 13 (1889) p. 5-36.

Beyond Bangui, Belgian explorers referred to the Ubangi river as the Doua-Kouyou,
and no longer felt bound by territorial agreements with France beyond the fourth
parallel. Vangèle records here how he was forced to withdraw in the face of Yakoma
resistance.

88 **Neu-Kamerun, Reisererlebnisse und Wirtschaftspolitische Untersuchungen.** (New Cameroon: travel experiences and an investigation into political economy.)
Emil Zimmerman. Berlin: Ernst Siegfried Mittler, 1913. 135p.

In 1911, Germany asked France to hand over all of French Congo (which, since 1910, had taken the name of French Equatorial Africa) in exchange for Germany's abandonment of its claims on Morocco. Germany finally obtained only a part of the territory of Moyen-Congo, Ubangi-Shari and Gabon. The author recounts his journey to the areas annexed by Germany, which had been given the name of 'Neu Kamerun'.

Flora and Fauna

89 **Contribution aux études ethno-botaniques et floristiques en RCA.** (A contribution to ethno-botanical and floristic studies in the CAR.) L. Aki Assi. Paris: ACCT, 1985. 139p.

This publication provides a valuable and substantial study of Central African flora. Reference is made to the names of the various plants and their uses.

90 **Etude sur les forêts de l'Afrique équatoriale française et du Cameroun.** (A study of the forests of French Equatorial Africa and Cameroon.) A. Aubreville. *Bulletin Scientifique de la Section Technique d'Agriculture Tropicale*, no. 2 (1948), 132p.

This work contains a phytogeographic sketch of the large forests of central Africa.

91 **Climat, forêts et désertification de l'Afrique tropicale.** (Climate, forests and the desertification of tropical Africa.) A. Aubreville. Paris: Société des études géographiques, maritimes et coloniales, 1949. 351p.

Aubreville expresses alarm about both the disappearance of forested regions, notably in the then French Equatorial Africa, and the impoverishment of the savanna soils.

92 **Les caféiers sauvages en Centrafique.** (The wild coffee trees in Central Africa.) J. Berthaud, J.L. Guillaumet. *Café, Cacao, Thé*, vol. 22, no. 3. (July-September 1978), p. 171-86.

Contains information on investigations carried out under the aegis of the IRCC and ORSTOM in January-February 1975. The research team was looking for, and trying to collect specimens of, the 'river coffee tree' (coffea congensis). As a result the structure and variability of the species was discovered.

93 **Etude du mileu naturel d'une région tropicale humide et suivi de son évolution saisonnière au moyen de l'imagerie Spot.** (The study of the natural environment of a humid tropical region and an investigation of its seasonal evolution using Spot imagery.)
Yves Boulvert. Bangui: (PEPS no. 186). ORSTOM-CNES, 1987. 25p.

This article includes twelve plates and twelve photographs in its presentation of the use of satellite Spot imagery to determine the seasonal evolution of the environment in the Central African Republic.

94 **Catalogue de la flore de Centrafrique. Ecologie sommaire.** (A catalogue of the flora of central Africa: basic ecology.)
Yves Boulvert. Paris: ORSTOM, 1977. 3 vols. maps.

This provisional catalogue contains the distribution maps (drawn to a scale of 1:5,000,000), of seventy known species of plants throughout central African territory.

95 **Végétation forestière des savanes centrafricaines.** (Forest vegetation in the Central African savanna.)
Yves Boulvert. *Bois et Forêts des Tropiques*, no. 191 (May-June 1980), p. 21–46. 18 maps.

The Central African Republic is situated at the point where the frontiers of the Guinea, Congo and Sudan regions meet. Corresponding with decreasing rainfall as one proceeds northwards, the vegetation changes from dense humid forest to thick undergrowth from southwest to northeast. Savannas cover four-fifths of the territory and can be subdivided into four areas: the Guinea-Congo area; a transitional Guinea-Congo area; a mid-Sudanese area; and the beginning of the Sudanese-Sahelian area. Species of trees and shrubs usually extend over two or three of these areas.

96 **Les principaux animaux de chasse de l'Afrique noire continentale française.** (The main animals hunted in mainland French black Africa.)
Pierre Bourgoin. Lorient, France: Editions de Bretagne, 1949. 246p.

The author, a gamewarden in Ubangi, provides a well-documented catalogue of the animal species hunted in central Africa.

97 **Sur l'existence d'une forêt vierge sèche sur de grandes étendues aux confins des bassins de l'Oubangui, du haut-Chari et du Nil (Bahr el Ghazal).** (The existence of large areas of dry virgin forest on the borders of the Ubangi, the Upper-Shari and the Nile river basins.)
Auguste Chevalier. Paris: Comptes Rendus de l'Académie des Sciences (5 March 1951).

During his exploration of Ubangi and Shari in 1902, Auguste Chevalier believed that the vegetation of the various zones of the colony (Guinean, Sudanese and Sahelian) was 'natural and primary'. Later he acknowledged that the land, cleared for cultivation hundreds of times and abandoned to bush fires, should be considered as fallow land. In 1950, during a journey carried out in the company of Sillans in the east of the area of Ubangi, he discovered huge areas of dry dense forest. These forests contained trees which had properties which enabled them to withstand the ravages of bush fires that burned during the dry season.

98 **Les moustiques de la République Centrafricaine.** (The mosquitoes of the Central African Republic.)
R. Cordella, Bernard Geoffray. Paris: ORSTOM, 1976. 106p.

The authors point out that the study of the various species of mosquitoes of the Central African Republic is essential for the development of a health policy.

99 **Grands fauves d'Afrique.** (Wild animals of Africa.)
Emile Gromier. Paris: Amiot-Dumont, 1950. 289p.

The author, an expert on the fauna of Upper Shangi and Upper Ubangi, provides an account of the natural habits of the rhinoceros, buffalo and lion of central Africa.

100 **La vie des animaux sauvages de l'Afrique.** (The life of Africa's wild animals.)
Emile Gromier. Paris: Payot, 1948. 343p.

Provides a solid documentation of the wild animals of Africa and especially central Africa.

101 **Vocabulaire botanique comparé de quatre flores vernaculaires de l'Empire Centrafricain.** (A comparative botanical vocabulary of four vernacular species of plants in the Central African Empire.)
Mission Sociologique du Haut Oubangui. Paris: Recherches Oubanguiennes no. 7, Labethno, Université de Paris X, 1978. 109p. éditions provisoire.

Presents provisional lists of the flora of the Ubangi aimed at sociologists carrying out research on the Zande, Nzakara, Ngbandi and Gbaya societies, with reference to Banda nomenclature, established by Father Tisserant in his *Catalogue de la flore de l'Oubangi-Chari* (q.v.).

102 **Les plantes chez les pygmées Aka et les Monzombo de la Lobaye (Centrafrique). Etude ethno-botanique comparative chez des chasseurs-cueilleurs et des pêcheurs-cultivateurs dans un même milieu végétal.** (The plants of the Aka pygmies and the Monzombo of the Lobaye [central Africa]. A comparative ethno-botanical study of the hunters-gatherers and the fishermen-farmers in the same plant environment.)
Elisabeth Motte. Paris: SELAF, 1980. 539p. bibliog.

This is a collection of studies and nos. 80-82 are of particular relevance to the Central African Republic. The author, a graduate in pharmacy and ethnology, devotes more than 100 pages to phytonomy (citing more than 600 species). Another 100 pages concern the use of the plants in the daily life of the populations concerned. Medicine and pharmacopoeia occupy some 120 pages. There is also a bibliography of more than 150 titles, as well as a rich index and lexicon.

103 **La faune de l'Equateur africain français, tome I oiseaux, tome II mammifères.** (The animals of the French African Equator, vol. I birds, vol. II mammals.)
René Malbrant, A. Maclatchy. Paris: Paul Lechavalier, 1949. 449p.
A basic work on the animals of the former French Equatorial Africa.

104 **Les savanes de l'Afrique centrale. Essai sur la physionomie, la structure et le dynamisme des formations végétales ligneuses des régions sèches de la République Cenrafricaine.** (The savannas of central Africa: an essay on the physiognomy, structure and dynamism of the woody plant formations of the dry areas of the Central African Republic.)
Roger Sillans. Paris: Editions Paul Lechevalier, 1958. 423p.
(Encyclopédie Biologique XV.)
According to this student of the botanist, Auguste Chevalier, at one time dense humid forest covered all of Upper Ubangi. The author asserts that the main reason for the disappearance of the forest was that trees were felled and the land cleared for agricultural cultivation; bush fires played only a small part in the dessimation of the forests.

105 **Catalogue de la flore de l'Oubangui-Chari.** (Catalogue of the flora of Ubangi-Shari.)
R. P. Charles Tisserant. Brazzaville: Institut d'Etudes Centrafricaines, 1950; Toulouse, France: Imprimerie Julia, 1950. 166p. (Mémoires de l'Institut d'Etudes Centrafricains, no. 2).
The author, one of Ubangi's first Catholic missionaries, was also its first botanist. He was in charge of the research centre in Boukoko.

Atlas de la République Centrafricaine. (Atlas of the Central African Republic.)
See item no. 9.

Plantes alimentaires du pays banda. (Food plants in the Banda region.)
See item no. 420.

Le caféier excelsa en République Centrafricaine. (The excelsa coffee tree in the Central African Republic.)
See item no. 427.

Agroclimatologie du Centrafrique. (Agroclimatology of Central Africa.)
See item no. 432.

Manual of forest botany. Tropical Africa.
See item no. 437.

Peoples

106 **Les grands mouvements de peuples en Afrique.** (The huge movement of peoples in Africa.)
Capitaine Avelot. Bulletin de Géographie Historique et Descriptive (1912), p. 75-216.
The author presents diverse theories regarding migrations in central Africa, laying emphasis on the Fang people (Pahouin) who left the Upper Sangha savanna to settle in the equatorial forests of Gabon. Also dealt with are the migrations caused by slave hunts.

107 **Pygmées de Centrafrique, ethnologie, histoire et linguistique.** (The pygmies of central Africa: ethnology, history and linguistics.)
Edited by Serge Bahuchet. Paris: SELAF, 1979. 179p. 8 maps. bibliog. (Bibliothèque 73-74, Etudes Pygmées III).
This volume is made up of five articles on the Aka pygmies of central Africa by Claude Senechal, Serge Bahuchet, Elisabeth Motte, Henri Guillaume and Jacqueline M.C. Thomas. It covers their language, pharmacoepia and relations with sedentary agricultural groups. The fruit of a long-term interdisciplinary project, it follows the publication of a phonology of Aka, and precedes that of an encyclopaedia, prepared collectively, and several specialized monographs. The volume ends with a bibliography of the principal publications on the four African pygmy groups: Aka, Baka, Mbuti and Twa.

108 **The Azande and related peoples of the Anglo-Egyptian Sudan and Belgian Congo.** P.T.W. Baxter, A. Butt. London: International African Institute, 1953. 152p. map. bibliog.
In spite of its title, this work considers several populations established in the Central African Republic north of the River Mbomu. The majority of the Zande population is found in Sudan or Zaïre, as a result of the borders fixed by the colonial agreements reached in 1894 and in 1899 between France, the Congo Free State of Leopold II, and the United Kingdom.

109 **Les Azandé. Introduction à une ethnographie générale des bassins de l'Ubangi-Uele et de Aruwimi.** (The Zande: an introduction to a general ethnography of the Ubangi-Uele and the Aruwimi river basins.)
A. de Calonne-Beaufaict. Brussels: Institut Solvay, Lamentin, 1921, 281p.

De Calonne-Beaufaict, considered to be the founder of Zande studies, lived amongst the Zande from 1905 until his death at Bondo in 1915. His friend, Colonel Bertrand, district head of Uele from 1909 to 1912 was able to collect only part of his numerous notes which he published in 1922.

110 **Les Bayas. Notes ethnographiques et linguistiques.** (The Bayas: ethnographic and linguistic notes.)
Marie-François-Joseph Clozel. Paris: J. André, 1896. 48p. map.

This brochure represents the very first study of the Gbaya population. Its author, the explorer Clozel, deceived by the multiple similarities between their respective civilizations, mistakenly classifies the Banda Yanguéré and the Mbomu amongst the Gbaya.

111 **Les Nsakkaras, leur pays, leurs moeurs, leurs croyances.** (The Nzakara, their country, their customs, their beliefs.)
Paul Comte. Bar-le-Duc, France: Imprimerie Comte-Jacquet, 1895. 136p. map.

This short book, written by one of the first French administrators of Upper Ubangi, forms the first study of the population of the kingdom of Bangassou. It consists of 30 pages of succinct notes, and about 100 pages of vocabulary and common expressions.

112 **Les Bandas de l'Oubangui-Chari (Afrique Equatoriale Française.)** (The Banda of Ubangi-Shari [French Equatorial Africa].)
R. P. Joseph Daigre. *Revue Internationale d'Ethnologie et de Linguistiques Anthrôpos*, no. 26 (1932), p. 647-695 and no. 27 (1933), p. 151-181.

Father Joseph Daigre, a Holy Ghost missionary in Ubangi since 1905, devoted his life to the Banda people. In six chapters, he gives a description of the people: their social conditions; the Banda family; religion; fetishism and superstition; as well as the flora and fauna of the Banda country. The article includes several very interesting photographs taken by the author.

113 **Les peuples de l'Oubangui-Chari.** (The peoples of Ubangi-Shari.)
Felix Eboué. *L'Ethnologie*, no. 27 (July 1933), p. 3-81; also published by the Comité de l'Afrique française, Paris: 104p.

Felix Eboué was an administrator for twenty-three years in Ubangi-Shari. He wrote the first complete study of the central African population. His work consists of three parts: the country and its people; ethnographic and linguistic studies; and local politics and economics. In the appendix there are also the lunar and agricultural calendars of the Banda and a vocabulary of the secret language of the initiated Bandas: Somalé or Sémali.

114 **Les Bayas de l'Ouham-Pendé.** (The Bayas of Ouham-Pendé.)
Felix Eboué, N. Simonin. Bulletin de la Société des Recherches
Congolaises, no. 9 (1928), p. 32-38.
The administrator, Felix Eboué, served in Bozoum in 1909-10. He provides some notes
on the Gbaya population of the Ouham-Pendé region.

115 **Les Mandja du Congo français.** (The Mandja of French Congo.)
Fernand Gaud. Brussels: Collection de monographies
ethnographiques published by Cyrille van Overbergh, Sociologie
descriptive et Institut international de bibliographie, 1911. 574p.
bibliog.
Fernand Gaud was assistant to the French administrator Georges Toqué in Upper
Shari in 1903-04, and helped him lead reprisal operations against the Mandja, who had
risen up against the colonial powers. It is not really a book but a collection of replies to
a sort of questionnaire, covering family life, and religious and intellectual life, as well
as the social life of the peoples in question. The basic vocabulary included in this work
remains the only published material on the Mandja or Manza language. The region
where this language is spoken is located at the centre of the Central African Republic
where the Ubangi and Shari rivers divide.

116 **Ethnographische Studie über die Baja.** (An ethnographic study of the
Baja.)
H. Hartmann. *Zeitschrift für Ethnologie* no. 39 (1927), p. 1-61.
The author, a German officer in charge of the post at Betare-Oya in Cameroon,
studies the ethnography of the Gbaya (the second largest ethnic group in the Central
African Republic), who found themselves under German administration at the end of
1911.

117 **Les Boffis de Boda.** (The Boffis of Boda.)
Lieutenant Hazard. *Bulletin de la Société des Recherches Congolaises*,
no. 20 (1935), p. 85-104.
Presents brief and specific notes concerning this small group in the Boda region, who
are part of the Gbaya-Mandja grouping.

118 **Exploration ranges of Aka pygmies of the Central African Republic.**
Barry Hewlett, Jan M.H. van de Koppel, Luca-Luigi Cavalli-Sforza.
Man, no. 17 (1982), p. 418-30.
The authors took part in interdisciplinary and international expeditions to the Central
African Republic, which have provided substantial information about the pygmies of
the southwest of the Central African Republic.

119 **The Gbaya.**
John Hilberth. Stockholm: Almquist & Wiksell, 1973. 143p.

The author, a Swedish pastor who spent forty years amongst the Gbaya of the Carnot-Berberati region, describes in detail the social and material life of this population.

120 **Histoires des peuplades de l'Uele et de l'Ubangui.** (A history of the tribes of the Uele and the Ubangi.)
Joseph Armand Hutereau. Brussels: Goemare, 1922. 334p.

This Belgian officer, who served in the Uele region from 1896 to 1909, returned in 1911-12 to undertake an ethnographic survey of the region. He was killed in the 1914-18 war before being able to collate his notes. Published in 1922, they give varied information about the populations settled on both sides of the Ubangi.

121 **Les Langbas. Population d'Oubangui-Chari.** (The Langba: an ethnic group in Ubangi-Shari.)
Suzanne Jean. Paris: BDPA, 1960. 93p.

An ethnological study carried out between April and December 1959, in eight villages in the district of Kembé. The author distinguishes two main groups amongst the Banda Langba: the Ngula and the Mabro.

122 **En Oubangui-Chari: le village baya traditionnel.** (In Ubangi-Shari: the traditional Baya village.)
Pierre Kalck. *Tropiques* vol. 55, no. 395 (May 1957), p. 67-70.

A brief note on the characteristics of the rural village in the Baya region.

123 **De l'origine des Bwaka (Ubangi).** (The origin of the Bwaka [Ubangi]).
Jean Leyder. *Bulletin de la Société Royale Belge de Géographie*, vol. 60, no. 1 (1936), p. 49-71.

The author, a Belgian magistrate in service in the Congo, studied the customs of this population who lived at the mouth of the Ubangi. He ascribes the Bwaka to the larger Gbaya group.

124 **Ligwa, un village zandé de la RCA.** (Ligwa, a Zande village in the CAR.)
Emile Leynaud. *Cahiers d'Etudes Africaines*, vol. 3 (1963), p. 318-50.

Emile Leynaud was a French administrator and head of the district of Obo. He presents here a study of Zande rural society in the early 1960s.

125 **Esquisse ethnographique des principales populations d'AEF.** (An ethnographic sketch of the main populations of FEA.)
Docteur L. Poutrin. Paris: Masson, 1914. 129p.

This work represents the first study of the various ethnic groups at that time listed in French Equatorial Africa and notably in the colony of Ubangi-Shari.

126　**The Azande: history and political institutions.**
　　　E.E. Evans-Pritchard.　Oxford: Clarendon, 1971. 444p. maps.

This book is a compilation of information from various sources, ranging over a century and including the author's own field research – covering the history and nature of the political institutions of the Zande of central Africa. It is an attempt to relate the development of their institutions and their historical experience, and to provide a framework for a consideration of the author's two earlier books on this people: *Witchcraft, oracles and magic among the Azande* (1937), and *The Zande trickster* (1967).

127　**Bondjo ethnicity and colonial imagination.**
　　　William J. Samarin.　*Canadian Journal of African Studies* no. 18
　　　(1984), p. 345-65.

On their arrival in the region of Bangui, the Europeans gave the name Bondjo to particularly hostile populations. This term was simply a form of the French word 'Bonjour', which had already given birth to the Sango expression, 'mboundjou' or 'mounzou', the white men. According to Samarin, the so-called Bondjo belonged to the Ngbaka Mabo ethnic group.

128　**A tribal history of the Western Bahr el Ghazal.**
　　　Father Stefano Santandrea.　Bologna, Italy. Editions Nigrizia, 1964.
　　　345p.

Presents documentary material on several peoples of central African origin (the Kresh, Kara, Binga, Yulu, Banda, Ndogo and Gola) who sought refuge in Bahr al-Ghazal.

129　**Ethno-geography of the Bahr el Ghazal (Sudan). An attempt at an**
　　　historical construction with a foreword by Professor Richard Gray.
　　　Father Stefano Santandrea.　Bologna, Italy. Editrice Missionnaria
　　　Italiana, 1981. 168p.

Father Stefano Santandrea left for the Sudan in 1937, where he zealously laboured for thirty years as a Catholic missionary, and as a keen interpreter of the history, culture, traditions and customs of the local tribes. This present volume is an indispensable adjunct to his earlier tribal history of western Bahr al-Ghazal (see previous entry).

130　**Die Baja, ein Negerstamm im Mittleren Sudan. Teil I: Materielle und**
　　　seelische Kultur, Teil II: Geistige Kultur. (The Baya, a Negro tribe in
　　　Middle Sudan. Part I: Material and spiritual culture, Part II:
　　　Intellectual culture.)　·
　　　Günter Tessmann.　Stuttgart: Strecker & Schröder, Part I, 1934. 244p.
　　　map. Part II, 1937. 180p. Re-published in 1985.

A member of the 1913 German expedition sent to the regions ceded by France to Germany, the author stayed in the Gbaya country for nine months, four of them at the post of Bozoum. His study, although hampered by the loss of a large part of his notes at the time of his deporation to Fernando-Po, remains the most complete work on Gbaya society. As it has never been translated into French or English, it remains unknown to the central Africans.

131 **Die Mbaka-Limba, Mbum und Lakka.** (The Mbaka-Limba, Mbum and Lakka.)
Günter Tessmann. *Zeitschrift für Ethnologie*, vol. 40 (1928), p. 305-52.
Some notes on the neighbouring populations of the Gbaya, peoples who, even today, are still rarely studied.

132 **Encyclopédie des pygmées Aka, techniques et langage des chasseurs-cueilleurs de la forêt centrafricaine.** (Encyclopaedia of the Aka pygmies: the techniques and language of the hunter-gatherers of the Central African forest.)
Edited by Jacqueline M.C. Thomas, Serge Bahuchet. Paris: SELAF, CNRS, LACITO, 1981-91. 5 vols.
The result of a meeting of linguists, anthropologists, naturalists and doctors, this collection of documents is a unique compilation of knowledge and complementary field experience. The encyclopaedia consists of four books, divided into seventeen volumes. The published volumes so far consist of a presentation of Aka society in all its aspects. The lexicons will consist of more than 10,000 terms collected in five different localities, each one accompanied by an ethnographical commentary.

133 **Les Azandé dans l'histoire du Bahr el Ghazal et de l'Equatoria.** (The Zande in the history of Bahr al-Ghazal and Equatoria.)
Arlette Thuriaux-Hennebert. Brussels: Institut de Sociologie de l'Université Libre, 1964. 318p.
In spite of its title, this work also concerns the Zande populations of the Central African Republic. It contains much information about the organization of the Zande states and the king's families.

134 **Moeurs et Coutumes des Manjas.** (The habits and customs of the Manjas.)
Antonin-Marius Vergiat. Paris: Payot, 1937. 326p. Paris: l'Harmattan, 1981. 344p.
The Manja ethnic group (Mandja, Mandjia, Manza) resisted Rabah the Sudanese conqueror as they had resisted the French. At the beginning of the century, they were required by the colonial authorities to transport goods between Ubangi and Chari. Many died undertaking this work. The author offers an in-depth study of these people who resemble the Gbaya. This work, re-published in 1981, remains the best study of a central African people.

Atlas de la République Centrafricaine. (Atlas of the Central African Republic.)
See item no. 9.

Histoire des peuples de l'Uellé et de l'Ubangi. (History of the peoples of the Uele and the Ubangi.)
See item no. 171.

La langue des Zandé. (The language of the Zande.)
See item no. 244.

Les rites secrets des primitifs de l'Oubangui. (The secret rites of the primitives of the Ubangi.)
See item no. 285.

Les sociétés primitives de l'Afrique Equatoriale. (The primitive societies of Equatorial Africa.)
See item no. 301.

Terre ngbaka. (Ngbaka land.)
See item no. 320.

Garçons et filles. Le passage à l'âge d'homme chez les Gbaya-Kara. (Boys and girls. The coming of age in the Gbaya-Kara.)
See item no. 324.

Prehistory and History

135 **Les martyrs de Bokassa.** (Bokassa's martyrs.)
André Baccard. Paris: Seuil, 1987. 349p. (Collection l'Histoire
Immédiate.)
The author, a French magistrate sent as legal adviser to President Dacko, lists the
crimes committed by the Emperor Bokassa. He gives a list of victims who were
arbitrarily arrested, often tortured and executed. It was essential that the truth be
known about this dark period of Central Afrian history. The summing up of his crimes
provided here is overwhelming.

136 **Ouaka 1900-1920.** (Ouaka 1900-1920.)
R. P. Ghislain de Banville. Bambari, Central African Republic:
Centre Culturel St. Jean, 1983. 101p. 4 maps. bibliog.
This work collates various little-known articles and reports concerning the history of
the region of Bambari, with particular attention to the resistance of the Banda Vidri
chief Baram-Bakié, to the French, and to the harvesting of rubber with its dramatic
consequences for the population. The text is accompanied by rare photographs of the
time.

137 **Recherches préhistoriques en République Centrafricaine.** (Prehistoric
research in the Central African Republic.)
Roger de Bayle des Hermens. Paris: Librairie C. Klincksieck and
Laboratoire d'ethnologie et de sociologie comparative Université de
Paris, 1975. 343p. maps. bibliog. (Recherches Oubanguiennes, no. 3).
Before 1966, when all the neighbouring countries had provided researchers with
numerous prehistoric finds, no systematic research had been carried out in the Central
African Republic. In 1967, the Natural History Museum of Paris, at the request of
President Dacko, put Roger de Bayle des Hermens in charge of a mission which
continued for two years. The discoveries were plentiful and of a high quality. The work
sums up these finds: Pre-Acheulian and Acheulian in Upper-Sangha; the Sangoan

36

complex in the Mbomu; Neolithic in Lobaye; quartz and quartzite industries in the region of Ndele; and rock art in Upper-Kotto.

138   **Quelques aspects de la préhistoire en République Centrafricaine.** (Some aspects of prehistory in the Central African Republic.)
Roger de Bayle des Hermens. *Journal of African History* vol. 12, no. 4 (1971), p. 579-97. 2 maps.
A résumé of the thesis written by the author after his three fruitful assignments in Central Africa in 1966, 1967 and 1968. The discoveries relate to prehistoric civilizations from the Lower Paleolithic to the Neolithic period.

139   **La traite orientale. Histoire des chasses à l'homme organisées en Afrique Centrale depuis 15 ans pour les marchés de L'Orient.** (The Eastern slave-trade: the history of the man-hunts organized in Central Africa for fifteen years for the Eastern markets.)
Etienne Berlioux. Paris: Guillaume, 1870. 350p.
In this documented study, the author shows how the establishment of Western commerce in Khartoum was followed by the intensification of the slave trade towards the East. It was these slave-hunts that led to the almost total disappearance of the border populations of Upper Ubangi and the Sudan.

140   **Notice historique sur la famille Abandia (branche Avourou Gobingué).** (An historical note on the Abandia family [Avourou Gobingué branch].)
Georges Binza-Hetman. *Bulletin de la Société des Recherches Congolaises* no. 8 (1927), p. 50-54.
This is basically a genealogical study of the Abandia, carried out by a descendant of the sultan, Rafaï.

141   **Français et Belges sur l'Oubangui.** (The French and the Belgians on the Ubangi.)
Marcel Blanchard. *Revue Française d'Histoire d'Outre Mer*, vol. 26 (1950), p. 1-30.
The author retraces the different stages of Franco-Belgian competition to explore the Ubangi river (1884-94).

142   **Le vieux Congo français et l'Afrique équatoriale.** (The old French Congo and Equatorial Africa.)
Henri Bobichon. Paris: Éditions Hérakles, 1938. 214p.
In 1897, Henri Bobichon, the colonial administrator, was given the task of ensuring that all supplies and equipment were available to enable the Marchand expedition to proceed from Bangui to Bahr al-Ghazal. This book contains Bobichon's memoirs.

143 **Bangui 1889-1989, points de vue et témoignages.** (Bangui 1889-1989, points of view and eye-witness accounts.)
Yves Boulvert. Paris: Ministère de la coopération et du développement, 1989. 310p.

On the occasion of Bangui's centenary, the author, at that time director of the ORSTOM centre at Bangui, collected several texts showing how the town appeared to explorers, journalists, people passing through and its inhabitants, be they European or Central African. Numerous illustrations are included.

144 **Points de vue nouveaux. Notes sur les origines et la fondation de Bangui.** (New points of view: notes on the origin and the foundation of Bangui.)
Jean Cantournet. *Revue Française d'histoire d'Outre Mer*, vol. 73, no. 272 (1986), p. 347-52.

This article put an end to several contradictory accounts of the foundation of Bangui. Using archive information, the author provides a thorough chronology and precise details of the successive locations of the post.

145 **En Afrique française, Blancs et Noirs, bourreaux et victimes.** (In French Africa, Whites and Blacks, torturers and victims.)
Pierre Cent. Paris: Imprimerie Henri Roberge, 1905. 52p.

Presents an indictment of the policies of Etienne Clementel, the Minister of the Colonies, and a strong defence of the Commissioner-General in the Congo, Emile Gentil. The latter had been severely criticized following the revelations made by the Brazza Commission of inquiry (1905) into crimes committed in the Congo and Upper Shari.

146 **Le Congo français, la question internationale du Congo.** (French Congo: the international question of the Congo.)
Félicien Challaye. Paris: Alcan, 1909. 311p.

The author, an associate professor of philosophy, was Pierre Savorgnan de Brazza's secretary, and was sent by the French government in 1905 to investigate the situation in French Congo. He describes acts of extortion committed in Bangui and in the Upper Shari. 'I fear', he wrote, 'that we will never be able to forget these miseries. All my life I will keep within me the sadness of having seen with my own eyes a living hell'.

147 **Un collaborateur de Brazza, Albert Dolisie, sa correspondance.** (One of Brazza's collaborators: Albert Dolisie, his correspondence.)
Charles de Chavannes. *Bulletin du Comité de l'Afrique Francaise*, no. 4.5 (1932), p. 219-37, 283-302.

Albert Dolisie, resident-administrator of the Lower Congo and Niari, gave instructions to establish a post at Bangui on 26 June 1889.

148 **Le Congo au temps des grandes compagnies concessionnaires (1898-1930).** (The Congo at the time of the large concessionary companies [1898-1930].)

Catherine Coquery-Vidrovitch. Paris: Mouton, 1972. 604p.

A carefully documented study of the pillage economy practised by the concessionary companies amongst whom almost all of the colony of French Congo (including the present-day territory of Central Africa) was divided in 1898. In spite of the scandals and the bankruptcies, the régime persisted until about 1930, when it was replaced by commercial societies which specialized in the import-export trade. For a well-documented analysis of the relationship between the concessionary companies and the colonial administrators see Jean Cantournet's *Des affaires et des hommes, noirs et blancs, commerçants et fonctionnaires dans l'Oubangui du début du siècle.* [Business and men, black and white, traders and administrators in Ubangi at the beginning of the century] Paris: Société d'ethnologie, 1992. 233p. (Recherches oubanguiennes, no. 10).

149 **Dar-Al-Kuti and the last years of the trans-Saharan slave trade.**

Dennis D. Cordell. Madison, Wisconsin: University of Wisconsin Press, 1985. 283p.

A good study of the Central African Republic by one of the most knowledgeable American scholars. This work is based on the author's doctoral thesis and analyses the role of the slave trade in the formation of such states as Dar al-Kuti in the northeast part of the present-day republic. Created by Bagirmi Muslim teachers and traders, this state was first a province of Wadai and then later the last, and largest, slave-raiding state in north central Africa.

150 **The Savanna belt of North Central Africa.**

Dennis D. Cordell. In: *History of Central Africa, vol. 1.* Edited by David Birmingham, Phyllis M. Martin. London: Longman, 1983, p. 30-74.

In this chapter, Cordell outlines the history of the northern savannas of Cameroon and the Central African Republic. After creating a coherent picture of the region's rich and varied ethnohistory, the author describes, in a sensitive and comprehensive fashion, the history of the region during the period of Muslim contact and the establishment of colonial rule.

151 **The northern republics, 1960-1980.**

Crawford Young. In: *History of Central Africa*, vol. 2. Edited by David Birmingham, Phyllis M. Martin. London: Longman, 1983, p. 291-335.

Describes the formation and development of the new independent states established in the region in 1960.

152 **Un ancien royaume bandia du haut-Oubangui.** (An old Bandia kingdom of the Upper-Shari.)
Eric de Dampierre. Paris: Plon, 1967. 601p. bibliog. 2 maps.

In this book, the author, a sociologist, has brought together a considerable amount of data on the old Nzakara kingdom both before the conquest and under French domination. The data is divided into ten chapters grouped into three parts: a desert in fifty years (depopulation and the fall in the birth rate), Nzakara society (notably lineage and the role of women), and the second conquest (the shock of colonization, and in particular the pillage of the concessionary companies at the beginning of the century).

153 **Des ennemis, des Arabes, des histoires.** (Enemies, Arabs, stories.)
Eric de Dampierre. Paris: Société d'ethnographie, 1983. 73p. bibliog.
(Recherches Oubanguiennes no. 8, Université de Paris X).

The author, using reliable sources and eye witness accounts gathered in the Nzakara country, tries to retrace Rabah's stay in the east of central Africa from 1876, as well as his defeat by the soldiers of the Nzakara king Mbari.

154 **The Nana-Modé, village site (sous-préfecture de Bouar, Central African Republic) and the prehistory of the Ubangian speaking peoples.**
Nicolas David, Pierre Vidal. *West African Journal of Archaeology,* vol. 7 (1977), p. 17-56.

The study of central Africa archaeological ceramics shows that the shapes and designs currently in use by the Ubangian-speaking population appeared in the first centuries A.D. This type of ceramics has been called Nana-Modé.

155 **Tazunu: megalithic monuments of central Africa.**
Nicolas David. *Journal of the British Institute in Eastern Africa* [now called *Azania*], vol. 17 (1983), p. 43-72.

The megalithic monuments situated between Bouar and Niem in the Central African Republic are known in the Gbaya-Kara language as *Tazunu* (upright stones). The oldest datings made, with the help of charcoal samples, by the Carbon 14 method, indicate that they were erected around 5490 B.C.

156 **Jean-Bedel Bokassa, "Emperor" of the Central African Republic.**
Samuel Decalo. In: *Psychoses of power: African personal dictatorships, 4.* Boulder, Colorado: Westview Press, 1989, p. 129-78, p. 200-05. bibliog.

The author sees in the Emperor Bokassa a characteristic example of a megalomaniac tyrant, rising up after the departure of the colonizer.

157 **Rabah et les Arabes du Chari.** (Rabah and the Arabs of Shari.)
Doctor J. Decorse, M. Gaudefroy-Demombynes. Paris: Guilmoto, 1968. 64p.

Recounts the adventures of Rabah according to Arab sources, with particular reference to his stay in central Africa from 1879 to 1891.

158 **Deux ans dans le haut-Oubangui.** (Two years in Upper Ubangi.)
Capitaine Devaux. Vichy, France: Imprimerie P. Vescenat, 1913. 78p.

The author, a French military officer and head of the area of Upper Ubangi, describes the military operations carried out from 1909 to 1911 against the populations in revolt in the regions of Lower Kotto and Ouaka-Kotto.

159 **Histoire militaire de l'Afrique Equatoriale Française.** (The military history of French Equatorial Africa.)
Commandant M. Denis. Paris: Imprimerie Nationale, 1931. 516p.

This account of the operations carried out by French troops proves that they were not simply deployed for the purpose of maintaining order, but that they were engaged in a real war of conquest with the aim of capturing territory valley by valley and village by village.

160 **Joseph Briand, médecin à Bangui 1898.** (Joseph Briand, a doctor in Bangui in 1898.)
M.C. Dias-Briand. *Recherches Centrafricaines, colloque de Senanque 24-25th September 1981 (Symposium of Senanque)*. Aix-en-Provence, France: IHPOM Etudes et documents, (1984), p. 51-71.

A collection of letters written by Dr. Joseph Briand, the resident doctor in the newly-established outpost of Bangui, at the end of the nineteenth century. These letters reveal the difficulties faced by Dr. Briand and represent an important historical account of Bangui in its early years. Also included in the work are comments on the letters by Briand's grandaughter.

161 **Le problème du regroupement en Afrique équatoriale française.** (The problem of consolidation in French Equatorial Africa.)
Joachim de Dreux-Brézé. Paris: Librairie Générale de droit et de jurisprudence, 1968. 211p.

An account of the breaking-up of the Federation of French Equatorial Africa and the attempts that were made to maintain cooperation between the four former colonies on the eve of their independence.

162 **La vie du sultan Rabah. Les Français au Tchad.** (The life of sultan Rabah: the French in Chad.)
Gaston Dujarric. Paris: André, 1902. 166p.

A biography of Rabah (b. ca. 1845) who was a strong military leader in the territory which now constitutes the Central African Republic. He conducted a multiplicity of wars against various ethnic groups. He was beaten by the French at Kousseri in 1900.

163 **Spécial Procès Bokassa.** (A special edition concerning the Bokassa trial.)
Elé Songo, édition spéciale. Bangui, 1987, 36p.

Provides an account of this public trial in 1986 which revealed the dark episodes in the reign of the Central African despot, Bokassa.

164 **Mémoire sur le Soudan.** (A report on the Sudan.)
Comte P.H.S. d'Escayrac de Lauture. *Bulletin de la Société de Géographie*, 4th series, vol. 10 (1855).

The work contains several pieces of evidence collected in the Sudan by a French diplomat concerning the populations of the Chadian and central African regions.

165 **Une étape de la conquête de l'Afrique Equatoriale Française, historique des opérations militaires de 1908 à 1912.** (A stage in the conquest of French Equatorial Africa: a review of the military operations from 1908 to 1912.)
State Major of the troops of Brazzaville, technical section of the colonial troops of the Minister for War. Paris: Imprimerie Militaire Universelle Fournier, 1913. 259p. maps.

This work, written by a group of French officers, details military action and objectives for the conquest of central Africa at that time.

166 **N'Garagba: la maison des morts. Un prisonnier sous Bokassa.** (Ngaragba: the house of the dead; a prisoner under Bokassa.)
Thierry-Jacques Gallo. Paris: L'Harmattan, Mémoires africaines, 1988. 159p.

A straightforward account, by a pilot-officer of the central African Air Force, of the daily struggle for survival in the sinister Ngaragba prison in Bangui.

167 **La chute de l'empire de Rabah.** (The fall of Rabah's empire.)
Emile Gentil. Paris: Hachette, 1902. 308p.

The administrator, Emile Gentil, Brazza's former companion, was district head in Ubangi and, in 1895, was given command of the expedition to Chad. With the help of reinforcements from Saint Louis and Algiers, Gentil destroyed Sultan Rabah's troops in 1900.

168 **Les débuts difficiles de la capitale de la République Centrafricaine: Bangui de 1889 à 1893.** (The difficult beginnings of the capital of the Central African Republic: Bangui from 1889 to 1893.)
Régine Goutalier. *Cahier d'Etudes Africaines*, 54, vol. 14, no. 2 cahier, Mouton et Cie (1974), p. 299-316.

The article explains how the small post of Bangui lived under constant threat from the villagers from the outskirts. Numerous night attacks and a climate of permanent insecurity often made it necessary to carry out harsh operations of retaliation.

169 **A history of the Southern Sudan (1839-1889).**
Richard Gray. Oxford: Oxford University Press, 1961. 219p.

The author brings to light the tight collaboration that existed in the Sudan between the European merchants and the Arab slave-traders, the effects of which were the renewal of slave-hunts in the Bahr al-Ghazal and the Upper Ubangi.

170 **Congo, terre de souffrances.** (The Congo, land of suffering.)
Marcel Homet. Paris: Fernand Antier-Montaigne, 1934. 253p.

Homet, a small-time French trader, experienced the hostility of the concessionary companies and the administration of the day. He was sentenced in Brazzaville for civil disobedience, and describes here the misery of the Lobaye villagers in 1932. This report had a strong influence on Barthelemy Boganda, the future deputy of Ubangi-Shari.

171 **Histoire des peuples de l'Uellé et de l'Ubangi.** (The history of the peoples of Uele and the Ubangi.)
Joseph-Armand Hutereau. Brussels: Goemare, 1922. 334p.

An ethnic analysis of the diverse riverside populations, most notably the Gbandi group.

172 **La question de l'Oubangui.** (The question of the Ubangi River.)
Marie-Jeanne Genneret. Louvain, Belgium: Université Catholique, mémoire faculté de philosophie et des lettres, 1962. 250p.

A study of the Franco-Leopoldian disagreement over the domination of the Ubangi River basin in the 1880s. The author provides a defence of King Leopold II's position in this affair.

173 **Etude sur le Dar Kouti au temps de Senoussi.** (A study of the Dar-el-Kouti in the time of Senoussi.)
Interprète militaire Grech. *Bulletin de la Société des Recherches Congolaises*, no. 4 (1924), p. 19-54.

Examines the history and institutions of this small central African Muslim state, which was placed under French protection in 1897.

174 **Mohammed ès Senoussi et ses Etats.** (Mohammed ès Senoussi and his States.)
Capitaine Emile-Pierre-François Julien. *Bulletin de la Société des Recherches Congolaises* no. 9 (1928), p. 49-96, no. 10 (1929), p. 45-88.

The military power of Senoussi, who accepted the French protectorate from 1897 to 1911, was supported by an impregnable commercial prosperity built on the slave-trade. This period in central African history saw the depopulation of the region of Upper Kotto become more pronounced, since it was subject to continual raids by the troops of the Sultan of Dar al-Kouti, a former vassal of Wadaï and Rabah.

175 **Histoire centrafricaine des origines à nos jours.** (Central African history from the earliest times to the present day.)
Pierre Kalck. Paris: Thèse de doctorat d'Etat ès lettres, Sorbonne, 11 June 1970, service de reproduction des thèses, atelier de l'Université de Lille III 1973, 4 vols. 1,777p. maps. bibliog.

The author, who served in central Africa as an administrator and adviser to successive presidents from 1949 to 1967, provides here an indispensable reference work. This thesis brings together almost everything known at the time about the history of the populations of the region and the events with which they were confronted.

176 **Les savanes centrafricaines au XIX siècle.** (The central African savannas in the 19th century.)
Pierre Kalck. *Histoire de l'Afrique Noire*, 1971, p. 191-199. In: *Histoire de l'Afrique Noire*. Edited by Hubert Deschamps. Paris: PUF, 1971, p. 191-99.

In this collective work, the author documents the hitherto largely unknown past of the populations of the central African savanna in the nineteenth century. These peoples were pursued by slave-hunters from the west, north and east.

177 **Pour une localisation du royaume de Gaoga.** (Determining the location of the Kingdom of Gaoga.)
Pierre Kalck. *Journal of African History* 13, 4 (1972), p. 529-48. map.

The author locates the vast kingdom of Gaoga, first reported by Leo Africanus in the sixteenth century, at the border of the Sudan, Chad and central Africa.

178 **Histoire de la République Centrafricaine des origines préhistoriques à nos jours.** (A history of the Central African Republic from its prehistoric origins to the present day.)
Pierre Kalck. Paris: Berger-Levrault. Collection d'Outre Mer, 1974. 343p. maps. bibliog. 2nd. ed. *Histoire centrafricaine des origines à 1966*. (Central African history from its origins to 1966). Paris: L'Harmattan, 1992. 354p. bibliog.

Traces the prehistory and the ancient history of the Central African Republic before examining the late 19th and 20th-century developments under the following headings: the era of the explorers (1885-99); brutal exploitation (1900-19); an abandoned colony (1919-39); Ubangian emancipation (1940-60); and the six troubled years which followed independence (13 August 1960). In the preface, Professor Hubert Deschamps asserts that this book is a classic work. The second edition contains a complementary bibliography for the years 1974 to 1992. This new volume has also been awarded the Georges Bruel Prize from the Académie des Sciences d'Outre-Mer.

179 **Barthélemy Boganda, tribun et visionnaire de l'Afrique Centrale.** (Barthélemy Boganda, a tribune and visionary of Central Africa.)
Pierre Kalck. In: *Les Africains*, vol. 3. Edited by Charles-André Julien. Paris: Editions Jeune Afrique, 1977, p. 105-137.

As a friend and adviser to this central African leader, the author was specially chosen to retrace the career and ambitions of Barthélemy Boganda, who disappeared in a mysterious air accident in 1959.

180   **Historical dictionary of the Central African Republic.**
Pierre Kalck, translated by Thomas O'Toole. Metuchen, New Jersey:
Scarecrow, 1980. 152p. Revised Ed. 1992. 188p.
This work, containing a detailed chronology, enables the researcher to identify the
important figures and events in the history of central Afria.

181   **Histoire centrafricaine, bilan et perspectives.** (Central African history,
assessment and prospects.)
Pierre Kalck. *Mondes et Cultures 42(4) Académie des Sciences d'Outre
Mer*, (1 October 1982), p. 813-24.
The author assesses historical research being undertaken at this time (ca. 1982) in the
Central African Republic for the Académie des Sciences d'Outre Mer (Academy of
Overseas Sciences.)

182   **La grande chronique de l'Ubangui.** (The great chronicle of the Ubangi
River.)
R.P.L. Lotar. Brussels: Institut Royal Colonial Belge, 1937. (Mémoires,
Section Sciences Morales et Politiques vol. VII-8). 99p.
Considers how, after having claimed all of the Ubangi River basin, the representatives
of King Leopold agreed to fix the border between the Congo Free State and the
French Congo along the course of the river, as far as the fourth parallel.

183   **La grande chronique du Bomu.** (The great chronicle of the Bomu
River.)
R. P. L. Lotar. Brussels: Institut Royal Colonial Belge, 1940. 163p.
(Mémoires, Section Sciences Morales et Politiques vol. IX-3).
From 1892 to 1894, the Leopoldians founded posts in the Mbomou River basin and in
Upper Kotto. The 1894 agreement with France forced them to retreat to the left bank
of the Mbomu. This river today forms the border between the Central African
Republic and Zaïre.

184   **La grande chronique de l'Uélé.** (The great chronicle of the Uele River.)
R.P.L. Lotar. Brussels: Institut Royal Colonial Belge, 1946. 363p.
(Mémoires, Section Sciences Morales et Politiques vol. XIV).
The 1894 Franco-Leopoldian agreement ensured that the Uele River basin, the true
upper course of the Ubangi, would be the territory of the Congo Free State.

185   **A History of the Arabs in the Sudan and some accounts of the people
who preceded them and the tribes inhabiting Darfur.**
Harold-Alfred Macmichael. Cambridge, England: Cambridge
University Press, 1922. 2 vols.
The author explains that Darfur appears to be the country of origin of several central
African peoples.

186 **Historique du poste de Bangui.** (A historical review of the settlement of Bangui.)

Stanislas Magnant. *Journal Officiel de l'Oubangui-Chari-Tchad*, (15 February 1907), p. 32-48, (15 April 1907), p. 92, (15 July 1907), p. 117, (15 September 1907), p. 119.

Studies the first years of this small French settlement founded in 1889 which is today the capital of the Central African Republic.

187 **Souvenirs d'Afrique. Tome II. Tournée d'inspection au Congo en 1908.** (Memories of Africa. Vol. II. A tour of inspection in the Congo in 1908.)

Général Charles Mangin. Paris: Denoël et Steel, 1936. 265p.

In 1908, General Mangin, a former member of the Marchand expedition, carried out an inspection, in Ubangi-Shari. He was highly critical of the concessionary companies operating in the colony at this time.

188 **La marche au Nil de Victor Liotard. Histoire de l'implantation dans le haut Oubangui (1891-1899.)** (Victor Liotard's march to the Nile: a history of settlement in the Upper-Ubangi [1891-99].)

Anne-Claude de Mazières. Aix-en-Provence, France: IHPOM, 1982. 164p.

As commissioner of the French government in Upper Ubangi, the naval chemist Victor Liotard occupied Bahr al-Ghazal in 1896. He was the driving force behind the success of the Marchand expedition in 1898.

189 **Les débuts du soulèvement de la haute Sangha en 1928.** (The beginnings of the uprising in the Upper Sangha in 1928.)

Marc Michel. *Annales du Centre d'enseignement Supérieur*, vol. 2 (1966), p. 33-49.

This article was written by Michel after he discovered administrative archives in Brazzaville relating to the origins of the so-called Kongo-Wara war. This war took the form of a general uprising of the Gbaya, and numerous other groups, in French Equatorial Africa against the colonizers.

190 **La mission Marchand (1895-1899).** (The Marchand expedition, 1895-99.)

Marc Michel. Paris: EPHE, 1968. 327p. La Haye, France: Mouton, 1972.

The central African population made strenuous efforts to enable the Marchand mission to reach the Nile at Fashoda on 12 July 1898. The Banziri supplied several hundred pirogues. The Dendi, Nzakara, Yakoma and Bougbou carried out the porterage as far as Wau, and about forty of them went as far as the Nile. The dismantling of the steam ship *Faidherbe* needed the help of 1,800 Yakoma and Sango. Considerable help was also afforded by the Bandia and Zandé kings.

191   **Une tournée en pays Fertit, Bria-Ndélé-Ouadda.** (A tour in the region of
        Fertit, Bria-Ndélé-Wadaï.)
        Capitaine Jean Modat. Paris: Editions du Comité de l'Afrique
        française, 1912. 207p.

The author, a French resident at Ndélé, the capital of Dar al-Kuti, went to the
settlement of Kafiakindji in the Sudan to meet the English administrator, Captain
Stoney. Modat's report of the journey provides an exceptional document about the
state of the region at this time.

192   **Le portage en Oubangui-Chari (1890-1930).** (Porterage in Ubangi-Shari,
        1890-1930.)
        Pierre Mollion. Thesis. University of Aix-en-Provence, France:
        IHPOM, 1982. *Sur les pistes de l' Oubangui-Chari au Tchad 1890-1930.*
        Le drame du portage en Afrique centrale. (On the trails from Ubangi-
        Shari to Chad 1890-1930: the drama of porterage in Central Africa).
        Paris: L' Harmattan, 1992, 272p.

The lack of communication routes other than the large rivers between the rapids meant
that the Ubangian population was used by the colonial authorities as porters (literally
carrying items on their heads). This was the way that administrative, commercial and
military transport was organised. The inhuman conditions in which this porterage was
carried out, especially in the Manja region, claimed numerous lives.

193   **Lettres de Maurice Musy.** (Letters from Maurice Musy.)
        Maurice Musy. *Revue de Géographie*, (Dec. 1890), p. 445-57;
        (Jan.-June 1891), p. 64-68, p. 130-33, p. 210-14, p. 291-94, p. 377-81,
        p. 454-55; (July-Dec. 1891), p. 42-65, p. 141-43.

Maurice Musy was a civil servant from the French Congo and head of the settlement at
Bangui from 15 September 1889 until his tragic death on 3 January 1890. Here he
describes in letters to his father all the difficulties encountered in setting up this first
French post in Central Africa.

194   **La guerre de Kongo-Wara (1928-1931).** (The Kongo-Wara war
        [1928-31].)
        Raphaël Nzabakomada-Yakoma. Paris: Thesis 3rd academic cycle,
        Université de Paris VII, 1975, L'Harmattan, 1986, 190p.

The so-called Kongo-Wara war ('War of the Hoe-Handle') or Baya war developed in
Central Africa from 1928 to 1931. Other ethnic groups from central Africa, Chad and
the Congo united with the Baya. The author tries to shed some light on this great
colonial revolt.

195 **Karnou, prophète de l'indépendance en Afrique Centrale** (Karnou,
     prophet of independence in Central Africa.)
     Raphaël Nzabakomada-Yakoma. In: *Les Africains*. Edited by Charles
     André Julien. Paris: Editions Jeunes Afrique, 1972, vol. 4. no. 48.
     p. 229–253.

The author rightly stresses the importance of Karnou, the charismatic leader of the
Gbaya revolt, the so-called Kongo-Wara war, waged against the French colonizers
(1928-31). Tracked down on 11 December 1928 by French forces, Karnou let himself
be massacred, as he had predicted.

196 **Jean-Bedel Bokassa: neo-Napoleon or traditional African ruler.**
     Thomas O'Toole. In: *The cult of power: dictators in the twentieth-
     century*. Edited by Joseph Held. New York: Columbia University
     Press, 1983. p. 95-106.

Presents competing hypotheses to account for the apparently aberrant behaviour of
this leader of the Central African Empire. The author speculates that the emperor,
though drawing directly on French-inspired forms and symbols, might better be
understood as a leader following local patterns of behaviour which had evolved as part
of the slave-trade along the Ubangui River in the last century.

197 **The 1929-1931 Gbaya insurrection in Ubangi-Shari: Messianic
     movement or village self defence.**
     Thomas O'Toole. *Canadian Journal of African Studies* 18 (1989),
     p. 325-49.

This article raises several questions regarding the participation of the Gbaya ethnic
group in a resistance movement against French colonial occupation. It suggests that,
rather than a religiously inspired rebellion, Gbaya participation in this 'war' might be
more correctly identified as self defence against European aggression.

198 **La question internationale de l'Oubangui (1884-1894).** (The
     international issue of Ubangi, 1884-94.)
     Paul Pauliat. Paris: Mémoire pour le diplôme d'études supérieures,
     Sorbonne, Paris 1966. 125p.

An analysis of the Franco-Leopoldian quarrels about the exact location of the northern
border of the Congo Free State.

199 **Bokassa 1er.** (Bokassa 1st.)
     Pierre Péan. Paris: Alain Moreau, 1977. 203p.

This is the first book both to denounce the crimes, embezzlement and bizarre
behaviour of the Central African dictator (crowned emperor in December 1977) and to
discuss the consequences for the country. The work was written by a journalist who
was at that time a top reporter for *Nouvel Economiste*.

200 **Description du royaume du Congo et des contrées environnantes.** (A description of the kingdom of the Congo and the surrounding countries.)
Filippo Pigafetta, Duarte Lopez, translated from Italian and annotated by Willy Bal. Publication de l'Université Lovanium, 1963. Louvain, Belgium; Paris: Editions Nauwelaerts, 1963. 249p.
A basic document for historians of the kingdom of the Congo in the sixteenth century, this work also covers the countries situated in the north of this kingdom (Anzica) and discusses their trade with the neighbouring regions of the Nubians.

201 **Entre Oubangui et Chari vers 1890.** (Between Ubangi and Shari around 1890.)
Christian Prioul. Paris: Université de Paris X, Laboratoire d'ethnologie et de sociologie comparative, 1981. 199p. (Recherches Oubanguiennes, no. 6).
An excellent study of the first years of French colonization in Central Africa and conditions in the country at this time.

202 **Conversation with Zobeir Pasha at Gibraltar.** Lord Ribblesdale. In: *The nineteenth century*, vol. 13. 1908, p. 936-48.
During this conversation, Rabah's former leader relates the two occasions that he stayed in the court of his father-in-law, the Zande King Tikima, the grandfather of the sultan Zemio.

203 **Neu-Kamerun.** (New Cameroon.)
Karl Ritter. Jena: 1912. 256p.
Provides German documentation about the territories handed over by France to Germany in accordance with the agreement of 4 November 1911.

204 **L'affaire du Congo. 1905.** (The Congo affair, 1905.)
Capitaine Jules Saintoyant with an introduction by Charles André Julien. Paris: l'Epi, 1960. 162p.
Presents the notes taken by this French officer who accompanied Pierre Savorgnan de Brazza, the French Commissioner General, on his tour of inspection of the French Congo in 1905. At this time, as Saintoyant's notes testify, appalling crimes were being committed in the Congo and Upper Shari. Saintoyant was also the author of an excellent multi-volume history of the French colonies.

205 **Histoire du bataillon de marche no. 2 de l'Oubangui-Chari (1940-1942).** (The history of the Foot Batallion no. 2 from Ubangi-Shari, [1940-42].)
R. Soriano. Beirut: Catholic Printing Works, 1942. 52p.
This brochure celebrates the participation of the central Africans in the fighting led by the Free French in the Levant, Libya and Ethiopia during the Second World War.

206 **Le ralliement de Bangui à la France libre – août 1940.** (The uniting of
Bangui to Free France – August 1940.)
Pierre Soumille, Pierre Mollion. *Ultramarines*, no. 3 (July 1991),
p. 3-15.
Using archive documents, the authors discuss the difficulties faced by General de
Gaulle in winning over Ubangi-Shari. Most of the French officers of the Bangui
garrison and some officials refused De Gaulle's call and remained loyal to Marshall
Pétain's government. Confrontation between the Vichy French and those loyal to De
Gaulle was only just avoided.

207 **Léopold II et la fixation des frontières du Congo.** (Leopold II and the
fixing of the frontiers of the Congo.)
Jean Stengers. *Revue Belge des Questions Politiques et Littéraires*
(1963).
The author denounces Leopold II's chicanery at the time of the fixing of the frontiers
of the Congo Free State at the European conference on African affairs held in Berlin
(1884–85). The frontiers were established at the expense of territorial losses on the part
of the other colonial powers.

208 **French colonization in tropical Africa (1900-1945).**
Jean Suret-Canale, translated from the French by Till
Gottheimer. New York: Univers Books, 1971. 636p.
The author cites examples of the colonial exploitation and pillage economy practised in
central Africa from 1900 to 1930. This book originally appeared in French in 1964 and
was entitled *Afrique noire occidentale et centrale.*

209 **Le mystère d'Agadir.** (The mystery of Agadir.)
André Tardieu. Paris: Calmann-Levy, 1912. 619p.
A history of the Franco-German rivalry in Morocco at this time which led to the
abandonment by France (1911) of a large part of the present Central African territory.
This land was returned to France by Germany as a result of the Versailles Treaty.

210 **The emerging states of French Equatorial Africa.**
Virginia Thompson, Richard Adloff. Stanford, California: Stanford
University Press, 1960. 608p.
Discusses what the author calls the 'Balkanization' of French Equatorial Africa.

211 **Les massacres du Congo. La terre qui ment, la terre qui tue.** (The
Congo massacres: land that lies, land that kills.)
Georges Toqué. Paris: Librairie mondiale, 1907. 288p.
In this book, the author, a colonial administrator, reveals the horror of a situation in
which he had been asked to be discreet at the time of the proceedings started against
him in 1905 in Brazzaville. He exposes how he was used as a scapegoat in order to
minimize the extent of the atrocities committed by the administration. He also
describes the bitterness of the combat led by the Manja people against the colonizers.

212 **Le voyage de mon fils au Congo.** (My son's journey to the Congo.)
Duchesse d'Uzès. Paris: Plon, 1894. 342p.

Elated by the anti-slave trade writings of the time, the young Duke of Uzès took
charge of a private expedition, which proposed to begin a real crusade against the
Sudanese Mahdi. The French colonial administration succeeded in using this mission to
subjugate the Bougbou of Lower Kotto.

213 **Vingt ans dans la brousse africaine, souvenirs d'un ancient membre de
la mission Savorgnan de Brazza dans l'Ouest africain (1883-1903).**
(Twenty years in the African bush, the memoirs of a former member of
Savorgnan de Brazza's expedition in West Africa, [1883-1903].)
Albert Veistroffer. Paris; Lille, France: Editions du Mercure de
Flandre, 1931. 241p.

The author participated in preliminary reconnaissance for the installation of the post at
Bangui.

214 **La civilisation mégalithique de Bouar. Prospection et fouilles 1962-1966.**
(The megalithic civilization of Bouar: prospecting and excavating 1962-66.)
Pierre Vidal. Paris: Klincksieck, Firmin-Didot, 1969; Publications of
the laboratory of ethnology and comparative sociology at the Université
de Paris X, 1969. 142p. (Recherches Oubanguiennes no. 1).

A doctor in ethnology, the author has been living in the Central African Republic since
1959. His study of the megalithic civilization of Bouar brings a new element to the
protohistory of central Africa. The variation in the suggested datings from 30 AD to
5490 BC poses problems that have still not been solved.

215 **A la veille d'Agadir. La Ngoko-Sangha.** (On the eve of Agadir: the
Ngoko-Sangha.)
Maurice Violette. Paris: Larose, 1914. 262p.

From 1906 onwards, the Ngoko-Sangha company under the influence of a shady dealer
called Mestayer worked an immense blackmail operation at the expense of the French
government. Mestayer and his accomplice, André Tardieu, took advantage of the
French government's fears concerning German ambitions in the Congo.

216 **Quinze ans de déstabilisation en Centrafrique. De l'action humanitaire
au dangereux précédent.** (Fifteen years of destablization in Central
Africa: from humanitarian action to dangerous precedent.)
Antoine Zanga. *Le Monde Diplomatique*, (April 1980), 12p.

Examines the nature of French military action launched in September 1979 in Central
Africa to dethrone the Emperor Bokassa.

217 **Réflexion sur les sources d'histoire centrafricaine: archéologie, traditions orales et autres matériaux.** (Reflections on the sources of the history of central Africa: archaeology, oral traditions and other material.)
Etienne Zangato. Master's degree dissertation, Université de Paris X, 1985. 238p.
The author consolidates the archaeological knowledge of the central African territory, particularly the northwest and the southeast.

218 **Histoire de la Centrafrique tome I 1879-1959, tome II 1959-1979. Violence du développement. Domination et inégalités.** (The history of Central Africa volume I, 1879-1959; volume II, 1959–79: the violence of its development; domination and inequality.)
Yarisse Zoctizoum. Paris: L'Harmattan, Bibliothèque du Développement, 1983-84. vol. I, 300p. vol. II, 383p.
With a preface by Charles Bettelheim, this PhD thesis from the Université de Paris V is heavily inspired by Marxist theories. Following an introduction on the slave trade and colonial military conquests, the first volume deals with: the appropriation of land by colonists; the period of pacification and the new forms of accumulation of capital; the beginnings of the development of agriculture for export; a new social differentiation; and the institution of neo-colonialism. The second volume is a general critique of the economy during the first twenty years of independence.

219 **Black ivory and white, or the story of El Zubeir Pasha, Slaver and Sultan, as told by himself.**
Translated and put on record by H.C. Jackson. Oxford: Blackwell, 1913.
The memoirs of Pasha Zubayr (Zobeir, Ziber), the main master-merchant of the Upper Nile, who took possession of vast territories in central Africa in the late 1850s, 1860s and early 1870s and who became Governor of Bahr al-Ghazal.

La République Centrafricaine. (The Central African Republic.)
See item no. 2.

Karnu, witchdoctor or prophet.
See item no. 272.

Le ralliement de l'Oubangui au général de Gaulle juin-septembre 1940.
(Ubangi rallies to General de Gaulle, June-September 1940.)
See item no. 372.

Six ans du gouvernement Dacko. (Six years of the Dacko government.)
See item no. 374.

Centrafrique. (Central Africa.)
See item no. 375.

Languages

220 **Le langage tambouriné des Banda-Linda (RCA).** (The drummed
language of the Banda-Linda, CAR.)
Simha Arom, France Cloarec-Heiss. In: *Théories et Méthodes en
linguistique africaine.* Paris: SELAF, 1976, p. 113-65.
The Banda's drummed language allowed for an astonishing circulation of information
over long distances.

221 **Les pygmées Aka et Baka: contribution de l'ethnolinguistique à l'histoire
des populations forestières d'Afrique Centrale.** (The Aka and Baka
pygmies: an ethnolinguistic contribution to the history of the forest
populations of Central Africa.)
Serge Bahuchet. Higher doctoral thesis in arts and human science,
Université de Paris V, 1989. 3 vols. 766p.
Bahuchet shows how the current refusal of the pygmies to learn the language of the
dominant ethnic groups has resulted in distancing behaviour. The conservation of their
mother-tongue assures the Aka and the Baka a privacy that prevents them from being
sucked into the dominant society, and provides them with cultural protection for their
spoken word is used as a 'secret language'.

222 **Dictionnaire sango-français, bakari sango-français et Lexique français-
sango, kété bakari sango-faranzi.** (Sango-French dictionary . . .)
Luc Bouquiaux, Jean-Marie Kobozo, Marcel Diki-Kidiri, Jacqueline
Vallet, Anne Behaghel. Paris: SELAF, 1978. 668p. (Tradition Orale
29.)
Sango, a language of the Ubangian group related to Ngbandi, is spoken by growing
numbers of people, as it has been chosen as the national language of central Africa. It
is already being used in the towns as the language of primary education and will
subsequently be employed in adult literacy programmes. This dictionary uses two types

53

of transcription, one being the standard transcription approved in 1967 by the Central African National Commission for the Study of the Sango Language, which unifies the various pre-existing orthographical systems, and the other being a phonological transcription.

223 **Etudes Yakoma, langue du groupe oubanguien (RCA). Morphologie – Synthématique.** (Yakoma language studies: morphology, word structure.)
Pascal Boyeldieu. Paris: SELAF, 1975. 152p. 2 maps. (Bibliothèque 47-48).

The Yakoma language, which is spoken in the Central African Republic on the left bank of the Ubangi River, is a member of a quite homogeneous block of languages which have given rise to Sango, the national language of the Central African Republic.

224 **Les langues fer ('kara') et yulu du nord centrafricain. Esquisses descriptives et lexiques.** (The Fer ['Kara'] and Yulu languages of northern Central Africa: descriptive outlines and lexicons.)
Pascal Boyeldieu. Paris: Libraire Orientale Geuthner (LAPAC) 1987. 280p.

The author expresses the view that the languages of the Kara and the Yulu, ancient populations of the northeast of the Central African Republic, are currently dying out and deserve to be safeguarded.

225 **Le 'possessif' en Zandé: 'parler au singulier'.** (The 'possessive case' in Zandé: 'speaking in the singular'.)
Margaret Buckner. In: *Singularités, Laboratoire d'ethnologie et de sociologie comparative, Université de Paris X*. Paris: Plon, 1989, p. 139-64.

A scholarly analysis of the semantics of the possessive case in the Zande language.

226 **La représentation et l'expression du temps en gbaya-buli.** (The representation and expression of time in Gbaya-Buli.)
Yves Cadiou. Paris: Université de Paris IV, 1980. 190p.

This typescript is a useful complement to the recent studies on the language of the Gbaya.

227 **Vocabulaire gnbwaga-gbanziri-mondjombo avec grammaire.** (The vocabulary of the Gnbwaga-Gbanzini-Mondjombo languages with grammar.)
R. P. Jean-Réné Calloch. Paris: Libraire Paul Geuthner, 1911. 204p.

A linguistic study designed for missionaries at the beginning of the century.

228 **Vocabulaire et éléments de grammaire français-gbéa, langue parlé de l'Oubangui.** (French-Gbéa vocabulary and elements of grammar, the spoken language of Ubangi.)
R. P. Jean René Calloch. Paris: Paul Geuthner, 1911. 170p.
This was the first study of a language that is very widespread in the west of the country.

229 **Le verbe banda.** (The Banda verb.)
France Cloarec-Heiss. Paris: SELAF, 1972. 136p.
Banda, the main language spoken by the savanna peoples, is the subject of an in-depth study in this book.

230 **L'Aka, langue bantoue des Pygmées de Mongoumba (Centrafrique). Introduction à l'étude linguistique – phonologie.** (Aka: a Bantu language of the Mongoumba pygmies. (Central African Republic.); an introducton to linguistic analysis – phonology.)
France Cloarec-Heiss, Jacqueline M.C. Thomas. Paris: SELAF, 1978. 204p. (Traditions Orales 28. Etudes Pygmées 11).
The Aka pygmies speak a Bantu language related to those of zone C (according to Gutherie's classification). This group of hunter-gatherers lives in the southwestern region of the Central African Republic along the Congo border.

231 **Dynamique et équilibre d'une syntaxe: le banda-linda de Centrafrique.** (Dynamics and equilibrium in syntax: the Banda-Linda language of the Central African Republic.)
France Cloarec-Heiss. Cambridge, England; Paris: Cambridge University Press, MSH, SELAF, 1986. 568p. (Descriptions de Langues et Monographies Ethnolinguistiques 2).
Banda-Linda is spoken near the centre of the Banda homeland, in the Waka Prefecture.

232 **Dictionnaire français-banda, banda-français et essai de grammaire.** (A French-Banda, Banda-French dictionary and grammar.)
R. P. Pierre Cotel. Abbeville, France: Editions Paillat, 1907. 60p.
This is one of the very earliest studies of the Banda language, the first vernacular language of Central Africa.

233 **Le français, le sango et les autres langues centrafricaines. Enquête socio-linguistique au quartier Boy-Rabé (Bangui, Centrafrique.)** (French, Sango and the other Central African languages. Socio-linguistic research in the Boy-Rabé quarter of Bangui, Central African Republic.)
Martine Deschamps-Wenezoui. Paris: SELAF, 1981. 187p. (Tradition Orale 48).
Bangui, the capital of the Central African Republic, is an ethnic and linguistic mosaic. The commercial and national language, Sango, is dominant in this urban milieu, but

Languages

French is an official language, used by the administration and for education. The main current trend is towards rapidly decreasing use of the vernacular languages (almost never used by the fifteen to twenty-five-year-olds), which are being universally replaced (even in family situations) by Sango.

234 **Le Sango s'écrit aussi . . . . Esquisse linguistique du sango, langue nationale de l'Empire Centrafricain.** (Sango can be written too . . . . a brief linguistic study of Sango, the national language of the Central African Empire.)
Marcel Diki-Kidiri. Paris: SELAF, 1977. 150p. (Tradition Orale 24).
Asserts that providing a language with a written form is an important process, for it detracts from the memorization procedures employed by the language-speakers.

235 **Eléments pour un manuel zandé, avec phrases, conversations et vocabulaire.** (Basic principles for a manual on the Zande language, with phrases, conversations and vocabulary.)
Norbert (Richard Walsh) Dolan. Averbod, Belgium: Imprimerie de l'Abbaye, 1912. 110p.
The author, who was a missionary at Tongerloo Abbey, wrote this as a practical manual for the use of Belgian missionaries and civil servants in the Zande region.

236 **Langues sango, banda, baya, mandjia.** (The Sango, Banda, Baya and Manja languages.)
Felix Eboué. Paris: Larose, 1918. 111p.
The future governor-general was, as this work testifies, a passionate ethnologist and linguist.

237 **La clef musicale des langages tambourinés et sifflés.** (The musical key to the drummed and whistled languages.)
Felix Eboué. *Bulletin de la Société des Recherches Congolaises* no. 28 (1941), p. 88-89.
This article is a summary of the studies made some years earlier by the administrator Eboué and his wife, during their time at the settlement of the Banda of Bambari.

238 **Sango, langue commerciale de l'Oubangui-Chari.** (Sango, the trading language of Ubangi-Shari.)
R. P. M. Gérard. Rome: Editions Sodalite de St. Pierre Claver, 1930. 111p.
This practical handbook contains a common vocabulary and the main grammatical rules of this lingua franca.

239 **Zande and English dictionary.**
Reverend E. C. Gore. London: The Sheldon Press, 1952. 309p.
A detailed lexicon by a Protestant missionary in the Sudanese Zande region.

240 **A Zande grammar.**
Reverend E.C. Gore. London: The Sheldon Press, 1926. 166p.
A scholarly grammatical study of the Zande language.

241 **Description phonologique du Mbum.** (A phonological description of the Mbum.)
Claude Hagège. Paris: SELAF, 1968. 68p.
The Mbum, a large population in the northwest of central Africa, have still not been the subject of a detailed study.

242 **La langue des pygmées de la Sangha, essai d'identification.** (The language of the Sangha pygmies, an attempt at identification.)
André Jacquot. *Bulletin de l'Institut d'Etudes Centrafricaines*, nos. 17-18 (1959), p. 35-42.
This is one of the first studies of the language of the Central African pygmies.

243 **Sango.** (Sango.)
Kerux-San Youen (Père Elzéar). Chambéry, France: Procure Mission 1950. 151p.
A practical handbook written by a Capuchin missionary.

244 **La langue des Zandé, vol. I: grammaire, exercices, légendes. Introduction historico-géographique.** (The Zande language, vol. I: grammar, exercises, legends. With a historico-geographical introduction.)
R. P. C. R. Lagaë, R. P. V. H. Vanden Plas. Ghent, Belgium: Editions Dominicaines Veritas, 1921. 248p. map.
The vocabulary consists of 1,003 words (of which 153 are of foreign origin). The sixty-five pages entitled 'Historico-ethnographical introduction' comprise a history of the Zande nation. The book also contains thirty-four pages of common phrases, seventy pages of grammar and eighty-three pages of tales and legends in the Zande language with their French translation.

245 **Vocabulaire de la langue baya (haute-Sangha).** (Vocabulary of the Baya language [Upper-Sangha].)
L. Landreau. Paris: Challamel, 1900. 56p.
This is one of the very first vocabularies of this language, and it was produced even before the exploration of the Gbaya region.

246 **Lexique comparatif des langues oubanguiennes.** (A comparative lexicon of the Ubangian languages.)
Edited by Yves Monino. Paris: Libraire Orientaliste Paul Geuthner, 1988. 152p. 6 maps. bibliog.

Eight linguists, seven of whom belong to the Centre National de la Recherche Scientifique in Paris, provide a summary of the current studies of the languages spoken in the Central African Republic. They offer a new classification in four groups, of thirty-four languages and dialects that have been retained: the Gbaya-Ngbaka group; the Ngbandi-Sango-Kpatiri group; the Sere Ngbaka Mbo group; the Banda group; and the Zande group. There is also a lexicon of the 204 most characteristic words.

247 **Introduction to Gbaya.**
Ph. A. Noss. Meïganga, Cameroon: Protestant Mission of Meiganga, 1973. 260p.

The author, a missionary's son, learnt to speak Gbaya and English concurrently.

248 **La langue des Aiki dits Rounga (Tchad-République Centrafricaine). Esquisse descriptive et lexique.** (The language of the Aiki called Rounga [Chad-Central African Republic]: a descriptive outline and lexicon.)
Pierre Noucayrol. Paris: Geuthner, 1989. 227p.

An interesting contribution to the study of the Rounga group which settled in the last century on the borders of Chad and Central Africa.

249 **Le verbe en gbaya. Etude syntaxique et sémantique du syntagme verbal en gbaya-kara-bodoe, République Centrafricaine.** (The Verb in Gbaya, a syntactic and semantic study of the verb phrase in Gbaya-Kara-Bodoe, Central African Republic.)
Paulette Roulan. Paris: SELAF, 1975. 187p. 3 maps. (Bibliothèque 51-52).

Kara-Bodoe, a dialect of the Ubangian language Gbaya, is spoken by more than 5,000 people to the southwest of Buar in the Central African Republic. The author precedes her linguistic analysis with a description of the Bodoe people (their occupations, social organization and beliefs) and their language (a classification and brief phonological discussion). This is followed by some methodological remarks.

250 **The Gbaya language: grammar, texts and vocabularies.**
William J. Samarin. Berkeley and Los Angeles, California: University of California Press, 1966. 246p.

The author was, for many years, a missionary in central Africa and today is the main specialist on the populations of the northwest regions of the area.

251 **A grammar of Sango.**
William J. Samarin. The Hague, The Netherlands: Mouton, 1967. 284p.

This work is one of the most complete grammars of the lingua franca of Sango, which has become the national langauge of central Africa.

252 **Basic course in Sango. Vol. I, Lessons in Sango. Vol. II, Readings in Sango.**
William J. Samarin. Lamoni, Iowa: Graceland College, 1967. vol. 1.
143p; Hartford, Connecticut: Hartford Seminary Foundation, 1967.
vol. II. 89p.
This text book provides a framework for the methodological teaching of the Sango
language.

253 **Sango, langue de l'Afrique centrale.** (Sango, the language of central
Africa.)
William J. Samarin. Leiden, The Netherlands: Brill, 1970. 146p.
Presents a summary of the main features of Central Africa's national language.

254 **Colonization and pidginization on the Ubangi River.**
William J. Samarin. *Journal of African Languages and Linguistics*, 4
(1982), p. 1-42.
An analysis of the earliest word-lists dating from the nineteenth century.

255 **Goals, roles and language skills in colonizing Central Equatorial Africa.**
William J. Samarin. *Anthropological Linguistics* no. 24, 1982. p. 410-22.
In this paper presented at the annual meeting of the Canadian Association of African
Studies in 1982, the author argues that due to the fact that Europeans were so few in
number and were not serious about banning indigenous languages, it was their African
soldiers and workers who communicated with the indigenous peoples and created
Sango.

256 **La communication par les eaux et les mots oubanguiens.**
(Communication by water and its influence on the formation of
Ubangian words.)
William J. Samarin. Paris: Table ronde ASOM, CHEAM, IHPOM,
1982. Aix-en-Provence, France: IHPOM, 1982, p. 172-239 (Etudes et
Document, no. 18).
Discusses the role of canoes and water transport in the creation of the Sango language.

257 **French and Sango in the Central African Republic.**
William J. Samarin. *Anthropological Linguistics* 28, (1986), p. 379-87.
Studies the respective roles of French and Sango.

258 **The colonial heritage of the Central African Republic: a linguistic perspective.**
William J. Samarin. *The International Journal of African Historical
Studies* vol. 22, no. 4 (1989), p. 697-711.
Considers the problem of language in Central Africa after the end of the colonial
period.

Languages

259 **Languages of the Banda and Zande groups: a contribution to a comparative study.**
R. P. Stefano Santandrea. Naples, Italy: Istituto Universitario Orientale, 1965. 251p.

Father Santandrea had a special interest in the Central African populations that had taken refuge in Bahr al-Ghazal near the Zande.

260 **A dictionary of Sango.**
Charles R. Taber, William J. Samarin. Hartford, Connecticut: Hartford Seminary Foundation, 1967. 338p.

The pastors Taber and Samarin combined their extensive knowledge of the Sango language to produce this dictionary.

261 **Die drei Sprachen des Bajastammes: To, Labi, Baja.** (The three languages of the Baya groups: To, Labi, Baja.)
Günter Tessmann. *Mitteilungen des Seminars für Oriental Sprachen zu Berlin*, vol. 34, no. 3 (1931), p. 70–115. [Afrikan Studien].

A study of the language that is currrently spoken by the diverse Gbaya groups and the two dead languages, one of which is still used, however, in initiation ceremonies for young people.

262 **Le parler ngbaka de Bokanga, phonologie, morphologie, syntaxe.** (The Ngbaka language of Bokanga: phonology, morphology, syntax.)
Jacqueline M.C. Thomas. PhD thesis, Sorbonne, Paris, 1963; The Hague, The Netherlands: Mouton, 1963. 308p. map.

An in-depth study of the Ngbaka language by one of the top experts on this ethnic group from southwest Central Africa.

263 **Dictionnaire banda français et français-banda.** (A Banda-French, French-Banda dictionary.)
R. P. Charles Tisserant. *Travaux et Mémoires de l'Institut d'Ethnologie*, vol. 14 (1931), 617p.

This basic dictionary deserves to be published in a new edition.

264 **Sango, langue véhiculaire de l'Oubangui-Chari.** (Sango, lingua franca of Ubangi-Shari.)
R.P. Charles Tisserant. Issy-les-Moulineaux, France: Les Presses Missionnaires, 1950. 272p.

Contains 45 pages of text followed by 227 pages of common French-Sango and Sango-French vocabulary.

Les pygmées Aka et Baka. (The Aka and Baka Pygmies.)
See item no. 221.

Les langues de l'empire centrafricain et l'enseignement des mathématiques.
(The languages of the central African empire and the teaching of mathematics.)
See item no. 454.

Religion

265 **Les missions catholiques et la formation de l'élite administrative et politique de l'Oubangui-Chari de 1920 à 1958.** (The Catholic missions and the formation of the administrative and political elite of Ubangi-Shari from 1920 to 1958.)
Maurice Amaye. PhD thesis, Université d'Aix-en-Provence, 1984; IHPOM, 2 vols.

The author compiled this study (867p.) while researching in France, using the documents of the different Catholic missions. He draws a positive conclusion about their activities.

266 **Vingt-huit années au Congo – lettres. Trente-six années au Congo – lettres. Quarante-quatre années au Congo – lettres.** (Twenty-eight years in the Congo – letters. Thirty-six years in the Congo – letters. Forty-four years in the Congo – letters.)
Monseigneur Prosper Augouard. Poitiers, France: Société française d'imprimerie et d'editions, 1905, 1914. 2 vols; Evreux, France: Poussin, 1921. 512p. map.

Monseigneur Augouard's stories must be read in the context of the conditions and beliefs at the beginning of the century. Their author shows himself to be conciliatory with the concessionary companies, despite their exactions, and severe with the Central African population, who were suspicious of the whites that had come to the country.

267 **Saint Paul des Rapides. Histoire d'une fondation (1894-1906). Recueil de textes.** (Saint Paul des Rapides: the story of a foundation [1894-1906]; a collection of texts.)
R.P. Ghislain de Banville. Bambari, Central African Republic: Mission Saint Jean, 1983. 140p.

With the concern for accuracy of a historian, the author has brought together diverse texts about the first years of the Catholic missions in the Central African Republic. The book contains a large amount of information about the 'civilizing' actions of the missionaries. The daily difficulties encountered by the founders of the Saint Paul mission near the small post of Bangui are described.

268 **Sainte Famille des Banziris. Histoire de la fondation de Bessou (Ndjoukou) par le Père Joseph Moreau (1894-1906).** (Sainte Famille des Banziris. The story of the foundation of Bessou (Ndjoukou) by Father Joseph Moreau [1894-1906].)
R.P. Ghislain de Banville. Bangui: Saint Charles, 1986. 201p.

The author has collected a series of eyewitness reports on the foundation, development and then abandonment of the model-mission of Sainte Famille. Letters written by its founder, Father Moreau, form a rare document for the history of Catholicism in Central Africa.

269 **En son temps, le Père Joseph Daigre (Oubangui-Chari 1905-1939): souvenirs, anecdotes et documents inédits.** (In his time, Father Joseph Daigre [Ubangi-Shari 1905-39]: unpublished memoirs, anecdotes and documents.)
R.P. Ghislain de Banville. Bangui: Saint Charles, 1988. 179p.

The author includes here two of Father Daigre's manuscript notebooks, in which the Banda region missionary describes tribal rivalries, the inhabitants' destitution, the exactions committed by the concessionary companies, and the abuses of power carried out by the administration. In addition, the missionaries' disappointments are also discussed.

270 **Les débuts de l'Eglise en RCA: notes et documents.** (The beginnings of the Church in CAR: notes and documents.)
R.P. Ghislain de Banville. Bangui: Saint Charles, 1988. 188p. maps.

This book is a review of the Central African Church's first century. It contains, for each of the country's six dioceses, statistics of the numbers of Catholics, biographies of the most noteworthy religious personalities paying particular attention to Barthélemy Boganda, the first Ubangian priest. Lists of the European missionaries and a table showing those who were ordained priests after Boganda are also provided. The book includes numerous illustrations.

271 **Itinéraire d'un missionnaire: le Père Marc Pedron.** (A missionary's itinerary: Father Marc Pedron.)
R.P. Ghislain de Banville. Bangui: Saint Charles, 1989. 241p.

A biography of one of the pioneers of the evangelization of Central Africa, based on his letters.

272 **Karnu: 'witchdoctor or prophet?'.**
Thomas Christiensen. *Missiology* no. 6 (April 1978), p. 197-211.
The author considers the personality of the leader of the Gbaya revolt of 1928 who was called a 'witchdoctor' in the colonial administration's reports.

273 **Nos Pères dans la foi. Les anciens de la mission Saint Paul.** (Our fathers in Faith: the elders of the Saint Paul Mission.)
R.P. Louis Godart, Cyprien Zoubé. Bangui: Saint Paul, 1986. 196p.
Describe the recollections of the founders of the Central African Church.

274 **Les Borossés. De janvier 1903 à avril 1915.** (The Borosses: from January 1903 to April 1915.)
R.P. Louis Godart. Bangui: Saint Paul, 1985. 192p.
The author explains the difficulties which his predecessor encountered in setting up the mission.

275 **De l'esclavage à la liberté. L'oeuvre de libération de la mission de la Sainte Famille.** (From slavery to freedom: the liberation work of the Sainte Famille Mission.)
R.P. Louis Godart. Bangui: Saint Paul, 1987. 211p.
The Sainte Famille mission provided an excellent example of rural development and transformation (see also item no. 268 above).

276 **Twenty-five years in Oubangui-Chari (1921-1946).**
Reverend Orville-Deville Jobson. Long Beach, California: 1947. 220p.
Presents the memoirs of one of Central Africa's most famous Protestant missionaries.

277 **Conquering Oubangui-Chari for Christ.**
Reverend Orville-Deville Jobson. Winona Lake, Indiana, 1957. 159p.
A useful work for gaining an understanding of the history of Christianity in Central Africa.

278 **Au coeur de l'Afrique. Le diocèse de Berbérati.** (In the heart of Africa: the diocese of Berberati.)
R.P. Le Kham. Annecy, France: Procure, 1969. 101p.
Entrusted to the Capuchin missionaries, this recent diocese of western central Africa is developing rapidly.

279 **Les soeurs spiritaines de Mbaïki et l'évolution de la femme en Lobaye (1931-1958).** (The Holy Ghost Sisters of Mbaïki and women's advancement in Lobaye [1931-58].)
Marie-Ange Kallanda. MA thesis, Bangui University, Bangui, 1987. 216p.
This thesis comes to the conclusion that the Catholic missionary nuns succeeded in emancipating numerous central African women.

280 **A l'ombre des palmes. L'oeuvre familiale et missionnaire des soeurs du Saint-Esprit.** (In the shadow of the palm trees: the family and missionary work of the Holy Ghost sisters.)
Sister Christiane Masseguin. Paris: Spes, 1942. 190p.
A summary of the work of the Holy Ghost sisters just before the outbreak of the Second World War.

281 **Prêtre blanc en Afrique noire.** (A white priest in black Africa.)
Abbé Joseph Perrin. Paris: Nouvelles Editions Mame, 1980. 206p.
A priest in the diocese of Langres, the author was sent to Cameroon then to Bangui during the regime of the Central African emperor. In his chapter 'Bokassa and the Church' (p. 115-27) he tells how Amnesty International asked him to participate in the denunciation of the tyrant's crimes.

282 **God in some of my valley days.**
Pastor E. Rosenau. Cleveland, Ohio. 1971. 79p.
When this volume appeared Pastor Rosenau of the Sibut mission was one of the oldest missionaries in central Africa, and exerted a tremendous influence.

283 **The black man's Burden: African colonial labor on the Congo and Ubangi Rivers, 1880-1900.**
William J. Samarin. Boulder, Colorado: London: Westview Press, 1989. 276p.
This book contains three chapters on the activities of missionaries (Protestant, Belgian and French) extending well into the twentieth century. The conclusion reflects on the significance of labour from biblical times to the mid-twentieth century in southeast Asia as well as Central Africa.

284 **Je voudrais voir Madame. La vie quotidienne d'une famille missionnaire [1958-76].** (I would like to see Madam: the daily life of a missionary family.)
Colette Steudler. Geneva: La maison de la Bible, 1979. 193p.
Describes the civilizing role of the missionaries and their families in central Africa.

285 **Les rites secrets des primitifs de l'Oubangui.** (The secret rites of the primitive peoples of the Ubangi.)
Antonin-Marius Vergiat. Paris: Payot, 1936. 308p.; 1951. 158p.
Reprinted: L'Harmattan, 1981. 192p.
The author is an expert on Central African traditions. The customs that he noted in the Manja and Banda groups are very close to those of the other main Central African groups. This is a work of seminal importance which seeks to understand the religion of the animist populations of former Ubangi-Shari. A detailed study of initiation rites is included.

Religion

Bibliographie signalétique sur les missions chrétiennes en Oubangui-Chari. (A descriptive bibliography of the Christian missions in Ubangi-Shari.) *See* item no. 513.

Population, Health and Welfare

286 Population size in African countries; an evaluation.
Centre français sur la population et le développement
(CEPED). Paris: The Centre, 1986, 1988. 2 vols.
Statistics on the populations of the various African countries, including the Central
African Republic, are provided in these volumes (363p. and 419p.).

287 Surmortalité méconnue du XVI siècle à la seconde guerre mondiale entre haute-Bénoué et Bahr el Ghazal. (The high mortality between the High-
Benue and Bahr-al-Ghazal from the 16th century to the Second World
War.)
Louise-Marie Diop-Maes. Paris: International network of
multidisciplinary research on history and prehistory in the Lake Chad
basin, Seminar ORSTOM, 1990. 18p.
An examination of the demographic decline in this part of the continent which extends
beyond the present-day border of the Central Africa Republic. The study is based on
data provided by Pierre Kalck in his higher doctoral thesis on the history of Central
Africa (1970).

288 Evolution de la politique de santé dans les Etats de l'Afrique Centrale.
(The development of health policy in the Central African States.)
Abel Goumba. Bordeaux, France: Faculty of Medicine, 1968. 347p.
7 maps. bibliog.
The author, the first leader of the Ubangian government, wrote this doctoral thesis in
medicine during his exile in France. It propounds a real programme of health and
social development, within the context of a global policy for the improvement of rural
life.

289 **Situation sanitaire de la République Centrafricaine en 1967. Etude générale et statistique.** (The health situation of the Central African Republic in 1967: a general and statistical study.) Abel Goumba. Rennes: Ecole Nationale de la Santé Publique, 1971. 380p.

Provides an important contribution to the study of the health situation of the Central African Republic in its first years of independence.

290 **Analyse des conditions préparatoires à la planification sanitaire en RCA.** (An analysis of the pre-conditions for health planning in the CAR.) Abel Goumba. Paris: Université de Paris I, Institut d'Etudes du développement économique et social, 1972. 138p.

Goumba stresses the need for advances in his country's economic development as the prerequisite for improvements in the nation's distressing health conditions.

291 **Essai d'utilisation des plantes médicinales centrafricaines.** (An essay about the use of central African medicinal plants.) Abel Goumba. Diploma of higher studies thesis, Ecole Nationale de la Sante Publique, Rennes, France, 1973. 253p. bibliog.

Professor Goumba has always been interested in African medicinal plants and drugs. These plants, often discovered by the pygmies, are widespread throughout the Central African Republic. They are bought by traders for the huge pharmaceutical laboratories abroad.

292 **Etude anthropo-sociale et généalogique de la population sara-kaba ndjindjo d'un village centrafricain.** (An anthropo-social and genealogical study of the Sara-Kaba Ndjindjo population of a central African village.) Georges Jaeger. *Population*, no. 2 (March-April 1973), p. 361-82.

After defining the biographical and anthropological environment of Miamane, a small village in the northeast of the Central African Republic, this paper puts special emphasis on the family, social structures, marriage, rules, fertility, and genealogies of its 393 inhabitants and their ancestors.

293 **Enquête démographique en République Centrafricaine 1959-1960. Enquête agricole en République Centrafricaine 1960-1961. Résultats définitifs.** (A demographic survey in the Central African Republic 1959-60 and an agricultural survey in the Central African Republic 1960-61: final results.) M. Lafarge. Paris: Ministère de la Cooperation, General Statistics Department INSEE, 1960, 1965. 2 vols.

These two volumes (262p. and 269p.) provide detailed results of the administrative census of the population of central Africa at the time of its independence, combined with an agricultural survey.

294 **Infécondité en Afrique noire – maladies et conséquences sociales.**
(Infertility in black Africa – diseases and social consequences.)
Anne Retel-Laurentin. Paris: Masson, 1974. 188p. 10 maps.
The author, a doctor of medicine and sociology, places venereal disease as one of the
main pathological causes of infertility amongst the Nzakara women. Retel-Laurentin
also comments on social factors: conjugal and pre-conjugal freedom; and above all the
abandonment of ancestral customs during the century of Bandia domination that
preceded colonization.

295 **Infécondité et maladies chez les Nzakara.** (Infertility and disease
amongst the Nzakara.)
Anne Retel-Laurentin. Paris: INSEE, 1977. 238p.
According to Dr Anne Retel-Laurentin, thirty per cent of the Nzakara women have no
chance of having a baby that is born alive, and only forty per cent have a chance of
having a baby that survives infancy.

296 **Un pays à la dérive. Une société en régression démographique. Les
Nzakara de l'Est Centrafricain.** (A country adrift. A society in
demographic decline: the Nzakara of east central Africa.)
Anne Retel-Laurentin. Paris: Encyclopédie universitaire Jean-Pierre
Delarge, 1979. 277p.
Considers the effects on the Nzakara of the fall in the birth rate which increased during
the colonial period.

**Aperçu bibliographique sur l'évolution de la population du centrafrique et de
sa capitale, Bangui.** (A bibliographical survey of the evolution of the
population of central Africa and of its capital Bangui.)
See item no. 327.

Bangui, capitale d'un pays enclavé d'Afrique centrale. (Bangui, capital of a
land-locked central African country.)
See item no. 344.

Social Conditions

297 **L'échange différé: esquisse d'une analyse comparative.** (Deferred exchange: a comparative analysis.)
Alfred Adler. Paris: Université de Paris X, Laboratory of ethnology and comparative sociology, in Singularités Paris, Plon, 1989. p. 369-400.

A comparative analysis of the 'exchange of women' in Africa, using data from the Nzakara. The words 'deferred exchange' in the title are used by sociologists to denote agreements made between different tribes to effect the choice of wives in order to bring about a balance. In this part of Africa a woman is regarded, above all as an instrument of work and if she marries into another tribe then compensation must be made.

298 **Péripéties des décisions en milieu rural centrafricain, impact sur le développement coopératif.** (The fluctuating decisions in rural Central Africa, and their impact on cooperative development.)
Benoit-Faustin Ato. MA thesis, Université de Poitiers, Poitiers, France, 1981. 365p.

Using the example of the Dakpa village of N'Gouya, 60 kilometres east of Kaga-Bandoro, the author attributes the failure of plans for socio-economic development to errors made by the technocrats, who were ignorant of local realities but who held political and administrative power. In his opinion, nothing can be done without the mediation of those traditionally in charge of village society. The book provides an excellent explanation of the mechanisms of this traditional power that has retained its enormous significance in the central African villages.

299 **L'anthropophagie dans le bassin de l'Oubangui.** (Cannibalism in the
     Ubangi River basin.)
     Monseigneur Prosper Augouard. Paris: Annales apostoliques,
     Congrégation du Saint-Esprit, 1890. p. 85-102.
The author who was nominated apostolic vicar of Ubangui in 1890, tells of cannibalism
among the riverside populations.

300 **Les villages de liberté en Afrique noire française (1887-1910).** (The
     freedom villages in black French Africa [1887-1910].)
     Denise Bouché. Paris: Mouton, 1968. 298p.
The 'freedom villages' where freed slaves lived, were areas originally set up by
Catholic missionaries around their first missions, and became real centres of
development.

301 **Les sociétés primitives de l'Afrique Equatoriale.** (The primitive societies
     of Equatorial Africa.)
     Docteur Adolphe Cureau. Paris: Armand Colin, 1912. 420p.
As assistant and then successor to Victor Liotard, Governor of the whole of Ubangi,
the author was one of the first observers of the societies in the eastern part of central
Africa.

302 **Penser au singulier.** (Thinking in the singular.)
     Eric de Dampierre. Paris: Société d'ethnologie, 1984. 43p.
This analysis, after the style of E.E. Evans-Pritchard, considers the soundness of
various aspects of Zande thought.

303 **Les sociétés d'initiés en pays banda.** (The initiate societies in Banda
     country.)
     Felix Eboué. *Bulletin de la Société des Recherches Congolaises*, (1931),
     p. 3-15.
Studies the various initiate societies in the region of Bambari and notably Semali.
These societies appear secret to the outside but are really 'traditional schools' in which,
for a specific period, the elders initiate young men and women in the village. They are
taught tribal customs, the rules of social life and beliefs etc. Thanks to these initiate
societies, the Central African peoples have been able to maintain their social cohesion.

304 **Evolution psycho-sociologique de la femme centrafricaine: l'élite future?**
     (The psycho-sociological evolution of the Central African woman: the
     future élite?)
     Patrice Endjimoungou. MA thesis, EPHE, Paris, 1975. 312p.
The authors believes that in Central Africa, as in the West, women are 'the future of
man'.

Social Conditions

305 **La vie rurale chez les Banda.** (The rural life of the Banda.)
Michel Georges. *Cahiers d'Outre-Mer*, no. 64 (October-December 1963), p. 321-59.
Considers the pace of life and agricultural conditions in Banda country.

306 **Pouyamba, village banda en savane centrafricaine.** (Pouyamba, a Banda village in the central African savanna.)
Michel Georges. Paris: BDPA, 1960. 2 vols.
This typescript is a monograph (151p.) about a village in the centre of Ubangi-Shari chosen for an experiment in rural development.

307 **Travail et changement social en pays gbaya (RCA).** (Work and social changes in Gbaya country, CAR.)
Gabriel Gosselin. Paris: C. Klincksieck Laboratoire d'Ethnologie et de Sociologie Comparative, Université de Paris X, 1972. 356p. 4 maps. bibliog. (Recherches Oubanguiennes no. 2).
This study was made in 1963 to examine firstly, the traditional collective organization of a population in the Ouham region, and secondly, the organization of agricultural work set up by the colonialists. Also covered here are the resulting social transformations and the attempts at pre-cooperative organization.

308 **Madomalé, village banda en savane centrafricaine.** (Madomalé, a Banda village in the central African savanna.)
Gabriel Gouet. Paris: BDPA, 1960. 74p.
Examines the conditions of rural life in a typical Banda village.

309 **Dario, village de haute-Sangha.** (Dario, a village of the Upper Sangha.)
Gabriel Gouet. Paris: BDPA, 1962. 2 vols. 160p.
A study of a rural locality in the West of the Central African Republic.

310 **Le mariage et la famille, chez les Gbaya (RCA).** (Marriage and the family among the Gbaya, CAR.)
Rodolphe Iddi-Lala. Paris: EPHE, 1969. 180p.
In this university dissertation the author describes the rules of marriage for the Gbaya people, who live north of Bossangoa.

311 **Contribution à l'étude de l'évolution sociologique en RCA.** (A contribution to the study of the evolution of society in the CAR.)
Rodolphe Iddi-Lala. MA thesis, Université de Paris X, 1971. 419p.
This thesis was carried out under the supervision of Annie Kriegel and presents a Marxist-Leninist analysis of the development of society in the Central African Republic.

312 **La mort sara. L'ordre de la vie ou la pensée de la mort au Tchad.** (Sara death: the order of life or the thought of death in Chad.)
Robert Jaulin. Paris: Plon, Collection Terre Humaine, 1967. 295p.

In charge of research at CNRS, the author stayed several times with the Sara from 1954 to 1959, and attended initiation ceremonies peculiar to this ethnic group from Chad and central Africa. The Sara rites are similar to those of the Gbaya and the Banda (initiated Labi and Semali societies). The concept of death amongst the Sara is completely different from the Western notion of death and the author emphasizes the distinction between 'harmful' death, which is wrongly called natural, and useful 'abstract and social' death, which is termed initiatory.

313 **Parenté et alliance chez les Banda du district de Bria.** (Relationships and marriage among the Banda of the Bria district.)
Emile Leynaud. *Bulletin de l'Institut d'Etudes Centrafricaines*, no. 7-8 (1954), p. 109-64.

The author, a sociologist and a French overseas territorial administrator, analyses the structures of traditional Banda society.

314 **Terre et pouvoir dans les populations dites 'Sara' du sud du Tchad.** (Land and power in the so-called 'Sara' populations in the south of Chad.)
Jean-Pierre Magnant. Paris: Université de Paris I, 1983. 735p. bibliog.

Analyses the relationship between land and power in the south of Chad as it applies to members of the same ethnic group living in the north of the Central African Republic.

315 **Repères sur la pensée centrafricaine d'aujourd'hui.** (Central African thought today.)
Jean-Dominique Penel. Bangui: Centre culturel français, 1983. 237p.

The author, at the time of writing professor of literature at Bangui University, is an expert on the younger generations of the central African people.

316 **L'enfant dans la société traditionnelle banda.** (Children in traditional Banda society.)
Fidel-Adoum Pickanda. MA thesis, Université de haute Bretagne, Rennes, France, 1981. 170p. maps. bibliog.

Emphasis is placed on the woman, who is viewed as the support for everything that concerns the child in Banda society. The Banda ancestral customs concerning childbirth and breast-feeding are described; the author then draws up a well-documented table of traditions which apply to growing-up and initiation, a major part of Banda life.

317 **La route Bangui-Kaga Bandoro. Structures héritées et mutations contemporaines dans une région de savane.** (The Bangui-Kaga Bandoro road: inherited structures and contemporary transformations in a savanna region.)
Jean-Louis Piermay. Paris: Université de Paris X, 1977. 312p.

The industrial cultivation of cotton has had a particular influence on the life of the populations of the zone studied.

318 **Oracles et ordalies chez les Nzakara.** (Oracles and ordeals among the Nzakara.)
Anne Retel-Laurentin. Paris: Mouton, 1969. 369p. bibliog.

Describes the customs and rites of these people which are similar to those reported by E.E. Evans-Pritchard among the neighbouring Zande.

319 **Réflexion sur l'évolution des chefferies traditionnelles.** (Reflections on the evolution of traditional chiefdoms.)
Jacques Serre. Paris: Centre des Hautes Etudes sur l'Afrique et l'Asie Modernes, 1955. 14p.

This brief study of the rôle of chiefdoms was written by a colonial administrator who was responsible for the districts of Grimari and Nola. See also entries no. 357 and 376.

320 **Terre Ngbaka. Etude des aspects de la culture matérielle d'une population forestière de la RCA.** (Ngbaka land: a study of aspects of material culture in a forest population in the CAR.)
Gabriel V. Sévy. Paris: SELAF, 1972. 410p. bibliog. Laboratoire des langues et civilisations à traditions orales.

Provides an in-depth ethnological study of the Ngbaka population of Lobaye.

321 **Le mariage dans l'Oubangui.** (Marriage in Ubangi.)
R.P. Charles Tisserant. *Bulletin de l'Institut d'Etudes Centrafricaines*, 2 vols. p. 73–102. (1951).

Tisserant was one of the first missionaries in the central regions of the Central African Republic. In this volume he examines the role of marriage in Banda society..

322 **Ce que j'ai connu de l'esclavage en Oubangui-Chari.** (What I saw of slavery in Ubangi-Shari.)
R.P. Charles Tisserant. Paris: Société anti-esclavagiste de France, Plon, 1955. 112p. map.

The author distinguishes the diverse categories of slaves that could be found in the past in central African villages: those taken in war; those captured by trickery or plunder; those enslaved through custom or by being slaves from birth; and those who were made slaves to pay for debts. Some information is included on the slavery of the pygmies and of women.

323 **Quelques remarques au sujet de la dot.** (Some comments about the
dowry system.)
R.P. Charles Tisserant. *Bulletin de l'Institut d'Etudes Centrafricaines*,
no. 4 (1957), p. 187-200.
Describes the rôle of the dowry which was linked to the traditional economic system.

324 **Garçons et filles. Le passage à l'âge d'homme chez les Gbaya-Kara.**
(Boys and girls: the change to adulthood among the Gbaya-Kara.)
Pierre Vidal. Paris: Université de Paris X, 1976. 382p.
The most diverse ancient societies throughout the world have identical concepts of
initiation rites, noted Claude Levi-Strauss. The author devoted more than twelve years
to a detailed study of the rites involved in the change to adulthood for boys and girls
amongst the Gbaya-Kara group in the region of Bouar. Although we already had some
information about the change with regard to the boys (Labi), nobody until this point
had revealed that of the girls (Bana).

Urbanization

325 **Les Kodro de Bangui: un espace urbain oublié.** (The Kodro of Bangui: a forgotten urban area.)
Marie-France Adrien-Rongier. *Cahiers d'Etudes Africaines* 81-83, 21, 1-3 (1981), p. 93-118.

The town of Bangui is divided into districts, which are like villages [the word for a village in Sango is Kodro], grouping together inhabitants of the same, or similar, ethnic groups.

326 **Recensement et démographie des principales agglomérations d'AEF. IV. Bangui 1955-1956.** (Population census and demography in the main towns of FEA no. 4. Bangui 1955-56.)
Edited by Laurent Bastiani. Brazzaville: High Commissionership of the French Republic in FEA, 1957. 17p.

This census of the town of Bangui was carried out in accordance with the French law of 2 August 1950. It concluded that at that time there were 72,000 inhabitants divided into six main groups representing more than two-thirds of the population (Banda seventeen per cent, Ngbaka ten per cent, Ngbaka-Mandja nine per cent, Mandja nine per cent, Gbaya nine per cent and Banziri seven per cent).

327 **Aperçu bibliographique sur l'évolution et la population du Centrafrique et de sa capitale Bangui.** (A bibliographical survey of population growth in Central Africa and its capital Bangui.)
Yves Boulvert. Bangui: ORSTOM, 1989. 10p.

Using published historical sources, the author traces the development of the town of Bangui since its beginnings as a small French post in 1889. The town's growth was particularly spectacular from 1950 onwards, and especially after 1970. From 39,000 inhabitants in 1950, the population of the Central African capital rose to more than 200,000 in 1970. In 1990, it reached 500,000 inhabitants, almost a sixth of the total population of the country.

328 **Quelques réflexions à l'occasion de la publication d'un article sur la ville de Bangui.** (Some reflections on the publication of an article about the town of Bangui.)
Yves Boulvert. Bondy, France: ORSTOM, 1986. 12p.
With reference to an article by F. Villien (see no. 342) on the town of Bangui, Yves Boulvert provides interesting details about the site on which the Central African Republic's capital is built, and discusses its expansion.

329 **Le problème du bois de feu dans les villages d'Afrique tropicale. Le cas de Bangui (RCA). Approche d'une solution agro-forestière.** (The firewood problem in tropical African villages: the case of Bangui (CAR); steps towards an agro-forestry solution.)
Bernard Cassagne. MA thesis, Université de Montpellier, France, 1987. 206p.
Discusses how the incredible growth in the population of Bangui has caused a problem of maintaining adequate fuel supplies for the town. Firewood is used extensively for cooking food and demand has outstripped supply.

330 **Bangui (Oubangui-Chari, AEF). Rapport d'une enquête préliminaire dans les milieux urbains de la Fédération.** (Bangui [Ubangi-Shari, FEA]: the report of a preliminary survey into urban environments in the Federation.)
Jean-Paul Lebeuf. Paris: Encyclopédie maritime et coloniale, 1951. 66p.
The author published this first demographic study of Bangui using the colonial population censuses of 31 December 1948 and 31 December 1949. On this last date the population was 39,267 inhabitants, 22,061 of whom were male and 17,206 female. He estimated, however, that the true figure for the total population could be as high as 60,000, if tax evaders were taken into account.

331 **Famille et résidence dans les villes africaines: Dakar, St. Louis, Bamako, Lomé et Bangui.** (Family and residence in African towns: Dakar, St. Louis, Bamako, Lomé and Bangui.)
Emile Le Bris, Alain Marie, Annick Osmont, Alain Sinou. Paris: L'Harmattan, 1987. 270p.
Presents a socio-anthropological analysis of each of these five urban settlements. The study focuses on: large families; residential systems; the community policies of urban areas; trade; and wealth accumulation.

332 **Le plan-directeur de Bangui.** (The master-plan for Bangui.)
Jean-Marie Legrand. *Industries et Travaux d'Outre-Mer*, no. 100 (1962).
Describes a master plan for Bangui which had been established as early as 1948 by a French architect and town planner, Fanny Jolly.

333 **La prostitution à Bangui: une étude de cas d'un phénomène social après 1960.** (Prostitution in Bangui: a case study of a social phenomenon after 1960.)
Agathe Ndoma. MA thesis, Bangui University, Bangui, 1960. 194p.
This is the only study of this problem which affects the capital's poorer classes and it was written before the appearance of AIDS in the town.

334 **Bangui, Central African Republic: a study in primary economic and social development.**
Thomas O'Toole. In: *Contemporary issues in African urbanization and planning.* Edited by R.A. Ubudho (et al.). Albany, New York: State University of New York Press, 1986.
The author indicates that away from the planned centre and its semiperiphery, the city is composed of spontaneously created African 'kodros' or villages. A single ethnic group often inhabits specific sections of the newer peripheral areas of the city.

335 **Shanty-towns in Bangui, Central African Republic: a cause for despair or a creative possibility.**
Thomas O'Toole. In: *Slum and squatter settlement in sub-saharan Africa: towards a planning strategy.* Edited by R.A. Obudho, Constance C. Mhlanga. New York: Praeger, 1986. p. 123-32.
Asserts that the city's future, like that of many urban areas in black Africa, seems to be bleak.

336 **Les mutations du milieu rural, à proximité de la ville, au nord de Bangui.** (The transformation of the rural environment, near the town, to the north of Bangui.)
Jean-Louis Piermay. *Cahiers de l'ORSTOM,* vol. 15, no. 2 (1978), p. 187-205.
Examines the changes to traditional society which have occurred as a result of the rural exodus towards the capital.

337 **Pouvoirs et territoire dans l'administration locale de la ville de Bangui (République Centrafricaine).** (Power and land in local administration in the town of Bangui [Central African Republic].)
Jean-Louis Piermay. *Recherches Géographiques* no. 18 (1981), p. 155-26.
Analyses the exercise of power in the administrative districts of Bangui.

338 **Alimentation, approvisionnement et agriculture à Bangui (République Centrafricaine).** (Diet, food supplies and agriculture in Bangui, [Central African Republic].)
Christian Prioul. MA thesis, Université de Bordeaux III, France, 1971. 2 vols.
An important study of the problems of maintaining adequate food supplies in Bangui, whose population now exceeds half a million inhabitants.

339　**Ville et agriculture vivrière en République Centrafricaine.** (Town and food agriculture in the Central African Republic.)
Christian Prioul. *Traveaux et Documents de Géographie Tropicale,* 7 (1972), p. 85-117.

The practice of agriculture in, or near, the town plays an important role in the budget of a large number of Bangui's inhabitants. Apart from the traditional small 'hut' gardens, 'hut' fields can also be found, mainly producing manioc. The growth of the town has also led to the creation of more distant fields. Market-gardening produces vegetables and this provides a good profit for the well-kept vegetable gardens.

340　**L'évolution de la propriété foncière dans la région de Bangui.** (The development of landed property in the region of Bangui.)
Christian Prioul. *Travaux et Documents de Géographie Tropicale,* 7 (1972), p. 955-68.

The town of Bangui benefits from a privileged situation concerning land ownership for the community possesses large areas of land which were given to it during the colonial period.

341　**Bangui. Evolution socio-démographique de l'habitat.** (Bangui: the socio-demographic evolution of the settlement.)
Marcel Soret.　Brazzaville: ORSTOM, 1961. 2 vols. 171p.

Thirty years ago the author studied population growth in Bangui but at that time he did not foresee the tremendous demographic growth that took place during the years that followed.

342　**Habitat et habitations dans les quartiers populaires: de Bangui.** (Housing and living conditions in the working-class districts of Bangui.)
François Villien. *Cahiers d'Outre Mer,* vol. 38, no. 151, (July-September 1985), p. 235-62.

Living conditions in this large rural town are still very precarious and diverse. Housing falls into three categories: permanent, semi-permanent, and land. The house is only one element of the family concession, which whether enclosed or not, includes a certain number of annexes.

343　**L'agriculture dans la ville: l'exemple de Bangui.** (Agriculture in the town: the example of Bangui.)
François Villien. *Cahiers d'Outre Mer,* vol. 41, no. 163 (1988), p. 283-302.

Agriculture is an important activity within the town of Bangui and indeed it is vital to the survival of the urban population. Cultivation normally takes place around the house, but it is also practised further away from the family residence.

344 **Bangui, capitale d'un pays enclavé d'Afrique centrale. Etude historique et géographique.** (Bangui, the capital of a land-locked central African country: an historical and geographical study.)
François Villien, Pierre Soumille, Pierre Vidal, Jean-Pierre Pirovano. Brazzaville; Bangui; Bordeaux, France: Universities of Brazzaville and Bangui and CRET Talence, 1990. 202p. bibliog. maps. (Collection Pays Enclavés, no. 4).
Written by four French teacher-researchers a century after the founding of the small colonial post of Bangui, this book provides a useful summary of many aspects of the history, development and current position of Bangui. It consists of four chapters: 'Prehistoric Bangui and the old population of the site and region'; 'Bangui from the founding of the French post in 1889 to the 1920s'; 'Bangui from the 1920s to today'; and a chapter covering the town's physical aspects and vegetation, its urban structure, its population and their activities, housing conditions and standard of living. Maps and photographs are included.

345 **Bangui, ruralité et citadinité d'une ville d'Afrique Centrale.** (Bangui, the rural and urban aspects of a Central African town.)
François Villien. Higher master's thesis, Université de Bordeaux, France, 1988. 1066p. bibliog. maps.
This study is divided into two parts. The first – 'The town and its population' – describes the history and geography of Bangui, the organization of urban spaces, outward expansion and the original ethnic groupings of its inhabitants. The second part – 'Man and his activities' – forms an excellent sociological and economic study, of both the working-class and modern districts. The town of Bangui is still growing, and now accounts for more than one-sixth of the total population of the country.

Bangui 1889-1989, points de vue et témoignages. (Bangui 1889-1989: points of view and witness reports.)
See item no. 143.

Politics, Law and Administration

346 **Politics and government in former French West and Equatorial Africa: a critical bibliography.**
J.A. Ballard. *Journal of Modern Africa Studies*, vol. 3, no. 4 (1965), p. 589-605.
The author explains the principal aspects of the constitution of the independent states in French Equatorial Africa in the 1960s.

347 **Pouvoir et obéissance en centrafrique.** (Power and obedience in central Africa.)
Didier Bigo. Paris: Karthala, 1980. 337p.
Financed by the Ministère de la Coopération, this study by a French war expert reveals the mechanics of power and obedience. It discusses the obstacles encountered in central Africa by the authoritarian regimes of Dacko and Kolingba and describes the monstrous and farcical image of Bokassa. In addition, with the help of constant references to central America, the author emphasises a classic African way of exercising power on the basis of patrimonialism, clientelism and theatricalization. Bigo made brief journeys to the Central African Republic and recounts the myth of Ngakola, and considers the career of David Dacko who was twice imposed as leader of the Central African Republic by France and abandoned power both in 1966 and 1981.

348 **Philosophie de l'opération Bokassa.** (The philosophy behind the Bokassa operation.)
Jean-Bedel Bokassa (et al.). Paris, Bangui: Central African République Press, 1973. 122p.
This panegyric, written by three of the emperor's ministers, praises the work carried out during the first seven years of Bokassa's reign.

349 **L'acte constitutionnel du 21 septembre 1979 et l'organisation des pouvoirs publics en République Centrafricaine.** (The constitutional act of 21 September 1979 and the organization of the public authorities in the Central Africa Republic.)
Jean-Marie Breton. *Revue Juridique et Politique, Indépendance et Coopération* (1980), p. 555-63.

Discusses the legal system which President David Dacko's French advisers set up in 1979 to replace institutions of the Empire before the establishment of a new constitution.

350 **La constitution du 1 fèvrier 1981 et la tentative de rénovation des institutions politiques en République Centrafricaine.** (The constitution of 1 February 1981 and the attempt to reform the political institutions of the Central African Republic.)
Jean-Marie Breton. *Revue Juridique et Politique, Indépendance et Coopération*, (1981), p. 867-82.

The constitutional proposals worked out by French lawyers were submitted to various socio-political bodies and the new constitution, which came into force after the referendum of 5 February 1981, marked the restoration, after twenty years, of universal suffrage. This constitution was, however, only in effect for seven months for when he took control of the government after President Dacko's resignation, General André Kolingba suspended the constitution (1 September 1981).

351 **La République Centrafricaine sans Boganda.** (The Central African Republic without Boganda.)
Capitaine André Bussières. Paris: CHEAM, 1963. 148p. (CHEAM Report no. 3822).

This French officer tries to draw a picture of the political situation in the Central African Republic in 1963, four years after the death of President Barthélemy Boganda. He makes peremptory judgements on the political personalities, and provides information about French policy on the country.

352 **Les lignes de force de la politique centrafricaine.** (The main themes of Central African politics.)
Capitaine André Bussières. Paris: CHEAM, 1966. 13p. (CHEAM Report no. 4079).

The author believes that Franco-central African relations were damaged in 1960 because of the dominant role played by the French High Commissioner, Paul Bordier, in choosing David Dacko as President Barthélemy Boganda's successor.

353 **Les mouvements du service civique en Afrique noire francophone: l'exemple centrafricain, Armée, Jeunesse et Développement.** (The movements of the civil services in black French-speaking Africa: the central African example, the army, youth and [rural] development.) Jean-Louis Chapuis. Paris: MA thesis, Université de Paris I, 1972. 218p.

President Dacko tried in vain, with the help of Israel, to start up a systematic military training for central African youth. His objective of establishing a 'pioneer year' which would enable young people to assist in [rural] development projects was short-lived.

354 **Barthélemy Boganda ou du projet d'état unitaire à celui d'Etats Unis d'Afrique latine.** (Barthélemy Boganda or from the plan for a unitarian state to that of a United States of Latin Africa.) Philippe Decraene. *Relations Internationales* no. 34 (Summer 1983), p. 215-26.

This article recalls the plan for the establishment of a United States of Latin Africa, which was worked out by the Ubangian leader, Barthélemy Boganda, who was President of the 'Grand Conseil' of French Equatorial Africa, between 1957-58. The text of the author's interview with Boganda in October 1958 is included, along with the declaration made in Paris on 14 January 1959, by Boganda, the first president of the Central Africa Republic, whose territory was, in the end, confined to that of the former Ubangi-Shari.

355 **L'Afrique Centrale.** (Central Africa.) Philippe Decraene. Paris: CHEAM, 1989. 154p. 2nd. ed. 1993. 191p.

The collection entitled 'Notes Africaines, Asiatiques et Caraïbes' and published by CHEAM, introduces the reader to a specific region. In this publication Philippe Decraene, director of CHEAM and professor of the History of the Civilization of Modern and Contemporary Africa at INALCO, examines the political and economic development of the ten states that form the sub-region of central Africa (Chad, Cameroon, Equatorial Guinea, Gabon, Sao Tomé and Principe, Congo, Zaïre, Rwanda, Burundi and the Central African Republic). Of particular interest is chapter 4 – 'République Centrafricaine – Deux immenses ombres' ('The Central African Republic – Two immense shadows'), p. 59-70.

356 **Le droit centrafricain de la nationalité.** (Central African nationality law.) Mandé Djapou. *Penant, Revue de Droit de Pays d'Afrique* (1978) p. 443, (1979) p. 59.

This law of nationality is largely based on French law.

357 **Circulaire sur la politique indigène en Afrique Equatoriale française.** (A circular on local politics in French Equatorial Africa.) Felix Eboué. Brazzaville: Imprimerie du Gouvernement Général, 1943. 38p.

Governor-General Felix Eboué (1883-1944) was for twenty-five years a colonial administrator who spent most of his career in Ubangi-Shari where he successfully oversaw the Kwango, Bambari, Bangassou and Bozoum districts. He joined forces with General de Gaulle on 26 August 1940 and was named Governor-General of French Equatorial Africa on 12 November 1940. Nobody knew the realities of Central Africa better than he and on 8 November 1941 he sent this famous circular on the local politics of French Equatorial Africa to all sub-division heads. The circular was very important for it was one of the principal working documents for the Brazzaville Conference in February 1944, which marked the turning point for the French African colonies. At the conference African leaders from French West and Equatorial Africa for the first time publicly called for reforms in French colonial rule thus starting the colonies on the road to independence.

358 **La formation de l'unité nationale en République Centrafricaine.** (The establishment of national unity in the Central African Republic.) François Guéret. MA thesis, Université de Paris I, 1970. 117p.

After the fall of Bokassa, Guéret became Minister of Justice, but subsequently resigned because he disagreed with the undemocratic policies of the new authorities. The author here investigates recent events, especially the political activities of Boganda, in order to provide an explanation for the political unity of the country despite its ethnic diversity.

359 **Circulaires de base (1952-1956).** (Basic circulars, 1952-56.) Paul Chauvet, High Commissionership of the French Republic in FEA. Paris: Imprimerie Officielle, 1956. 223p.

Governor-General Chauvet was placed in charge of the FEA in November 1951, and collated various circulars and sent them to the administrators in the hope that they would form the framework of new policies. He asked that they be read by the colonial civil servants when they took office, because along with the Eboué circular of 1941 (q.v.), they were considered to be fundamental. Of particular interest are p. 57-60, letter no. 1692 AP1 of 29 May 1954, addressed to the Governor of Ubangi-Shari, analysing the relationship between the Europeans and the Africans.

360 **Accords entre la République Française et les Républiques Centrafricaine, du Congo et du Tchad.** (Agreements between the French Republic and the Central African Republic, the Congo and Chad.) Journal Officiel de la République Française. Paris: The Journal, 1960. 27p.

The special agreements of 12 July 1910 reproduced in this booklet were approved by a French law of 28 July 1960. The Central African Republic was to gain independence on 13 August 1960.

361 **République Centrafricaine: entre les décombres et le redressement.** (The Central African Republic: between the rubble and recovery.) Pierre Kalck. *Le Monde Diplomatique*, no. 341 (August 1982), p. 16.

The author studies the situation of the Central African Republic in 1982 from three angles: the problems of the past; the nature of the problems; and the scale of the national recovery which needed to be organized. He concludes that the Central African Republic will be condemned to perpetual poverty if it does not become more outward-looking and is prepared to accept foreign aid from a country that knows how to avoid the errors that have been committed for more than twenty years.

362 **L'administration publique centrafricaine.** (Central African public administration.)
Francis Keller. PhD thesis, Université de Paris I, 1982. 486p.

This thesis consists of two parts. The first analyses the factors conditioning the system of public administration, notably the economic history of the country and its socio-cultural development. The second part describes the working of the system, which was copied from the earlier colonial administration. Current problems (i.e., ca. early 1980s) considered are: regional disparities; local sub-administration; and the human factor in the choice of managers.

363 **La constitution de la République Centrafricaine du 21 novembre 1986.**
(The constitution of the Central African Republic of 21 November 1986.)
Claude Leclercq. *Revue Juridique et Politique, Indépendance et Coopération*, (October-December 1987), p. 290-98.

Written by a French professor, this constitution was inspired by that of the Ivory Coast and established a presidential system of government and a parliament consisting of the National Assembly and the Economic and Regional Council. This constitution was passed on 21 November 1986, and was the eighth constitutional text promulgated since 1959.

364 **L'organisation judiciaire de l'Empire Centrafricain.** (The organization of the legal system in the Central African Empire.)
Fidèle Mandaba-Bornou. PhD thesis, Université de Paris I, 1977.

Compares the legal system in the Central African Republic with that of the former colonial powers. The author, who became a magistrate, omits to point out that the independence of the judges was purely theoretical under Bokassa's dictatorship.

365 **La militarisation des systèmes politiques africains (1960-1972). Une tentative d'explication.** (The militarization of African political systems [1960-72]: an explanation.)
Michel Martin. Québec: Naaman, 1979. 200p.

This book contains a comment on the seizing of power by Jean-Bedel Bokassa, a veteran of the French colonial army, on 1 January 1966.

366 **La nouvelle constitution centrafricaine de 1976. De la république monocratique à l'empire parlementaire.** (The new central African constitution of 1976: from monocratic republic to parliamentary empire.)
J. Owona. *Penant, Revue de Droit des Pays d'Afrique*, no. 759 (January-March 1978), 27p.

Describes the institutions of the so-called 'parliamentary' empire. However, everything discussed here remained at a theoretical level and did not correspond to the reality of the situation in the Central African Republic.

367 **Les institutions politiques centrafricaines.** (The central African political institutions.)
Jean-Jacques Raynal. Bangui: Ecole Nationale d'Administration et de la magistrature, 1982. 80p.

The author, a French academic on Voluntary Service Overseas in Bangui, outlines for the trainee administrators and magistrates in his charge the institutions in the Central African Republic following Dacko's resignation and the suspension of the constitution.

368 **L'évolution politique et constitutionnelle de la République Centrafricaine.** (The political and constitutional evolution of the Central African Republic.)
Jean-Jacques Raynal. *Revue Juridique et Publique, Indépendance et Coopération* no. 4 (1983), p. 795-816.

The author analyses the different constititions established at various times in the Central African Republic.

369 **La constitution centrafricaine du 28 novembre 1986.** (The Central African constitution of 28 November 1986.)
Jean-Jacques Raynal. *Penant, Revue de droit des Pays d'Afrique*, no. 798 (October-December 1988). p. 475-82.

In this article a French academic comments on the new constitution. The author dislikes the derivative nature of the central African governments and believes that the institutional history of the Central African Republic seems to have suffered a reversal because a consular regime has been established just seven years after the end of the 'imperial nightmare'.

370 **Un jugement coutumier n'zakara.** (A customary N'zakara judgement.)
Anne Retel-Laurentin. *Cahiers d'Etudes Africaines*, 11 (1963), p. 391-412.

The author discusses a customary judgement made in 1960 by King Bangassou's son, the head of the canton of Sayo. Apart from being an aid to our understanding of the laws in force in Nazkara society, this judgement also contains elements which are useful in understanding Nzakara logic, psychology and humour.

371 **Le parti unique en République Centrafricaine: le MESAN.** (The single party in the Central African Republic: MESAN.)
Jean-Pierre Rougeaux. Diploma of Higher Studies in Political Science thesis, Faculty of Law & Economic Science, Paris, 1968. 87p.

Considers the 'Movement for the Social Development of Black Africa' (MESAN – Mouvement pour l'évolution sociale de l'Afrique noire), created by Barthélemy Boganda in 1949. David Dacko completely changed the Movement, turning it into a single party which was maintained by his successor, Jean-Bedel Bokassa.

372 **Le ralliement de l'Oubangui au général de Gaulle juin-septembre 1940.**
(Ubangi rallies to General de Gaulle, June-September 1940.)
Jacques Serre. Mondes et Cultures. Académie des Services d'Outre
Mer, vol. 49, 2-3-4 (1989), p. 573-92.

Describes how at this time Ubangi united with Free French Equatorial Africa which
was allied with General Charles de Gaulle.

373 **L'Ecole Nationale d'Administration de la République Centrafricaine.**
(The National School of Administration in the Central African
Republic.)
Jacques Serre. *Revue Juridique et Politique, Indépendance et
Coopération*, (August 1964), p. 37-40.

Presents a brief survey of the Training School for Managers in the Public Service and
Central African Public Office, now known as ENAM. It is equipped with a library
containing a store of old archives.

374 **Six ans de gouvernement Dacko.** (Six years of the Dacko government.)
Jacques Serre. *Revue Française d'Etudes Politiques Africaines*, 117
(1975), p. 73-104.

The author, an adviser to the president of the Central African Republic, draws a
positive conclusion about the first six years of independence.

375 **Centrafrique.** (Central Africa.)
*SILO (Service International de Liaison et d'Organisation pour un
développement solidaire), Cahiers d'Information* no. 1, (October 1982),
38p. 22 maps.

After providing general information about the country, this booklet recounts the
political development of the Central African Republic, both before Bokassa seized
power, under his regime and after his fall. The reasons why France 'chose' David
Dacko, who was returned to the country by French parachutists, as the emperor's
successor are also explained.

376 **Felix Eboué and the chiefs. Perceptions of power in early Oubangui-
Chari.**
Brian Weinstein. *Journal of African History*, 1970. p. 107–26.

After investigating the places where Eboué was administrator for almost twenty-five
years, the author traces the origin of the Governor-General's theories about the local
chiefs.

377 **Le MESAN et le pouvoir en RCA.** (MESAN and power in the CAR.)
L. Yagao-Ngama. Paris: M.A. thesis, Université de Paris X, 1974.
471p.

The party was created on 28 September 1949 by Barthélemy Boganda who wished it to
be open to 'all the Blacks of the world'. His successors, David Dacko and Jean-Bedel
Bokassa, created a single party, and rapidly transformed the country into a party-state
modelled on the Soviet Union.

Economy and Transport

378 **L'évolution économique de la République Centrafricaine depuis l'indépendance et ses perspectives de développement.** (The economic evolution of the Central African Republic since its independence, and its prospects for development.)
Chantal Basquin. Paris: Ministère de la coopération et développement, 1986. 117p. bibliog.
After the disappointments recorded following successive plans for economic development in the Central African Republic, the author considers future objectives that could reasonably be expected to be achieved.

379 **Etude de la faisabilité du projet d'aménagement et d'organisation du transport routier sur l'axe Douala-Bangui.** (A study examining the feasibility of planning and organizing road transport on the Douala-Bangui axis.)
BCEOM. Paris: 1987. 205p.
Presents proposals to improve the international road traffic on this axis.

380 **Production cotonnière et développement: le cas centrafricain.** (Cotton production and development: the central African case.)
Jean Cantournet. *Marchés Tropicaux et Méditerranéens*, no. 2218 (13 May 1988), p. 1231-36.
Examines: the beginnings of the rapid development of cotton cultivation in Ubangi; the natural and human aspects of such development; the methods used; purchasing procedures; manufacturing; marketing; and the reasons for the fluctuation in cotton

prices. This article is written by the former director-general of UCCA (L'Union Cotonnière Centrafricaine) in Bangui.

381 **Une réussite d'agro-technique: la mise en route du complexe sucrier de la Ouaka (RCA).** (A success of agro-technology: the establishment of the Ouaka sugar complex [CAR].)
B. Cauchy. *Industries Alimentaires et Agricoles*, vol. 105, no. 11 (1988), p. 1149-52.
Details the introduction of sugar cane cultivation in the Central African Republic.

382 **La Zone Franc (Rapports Annuels par Etat).** (The Franc Area: Annual Reports state by state.)
Comité monétaire de la zone franc. Paris: Banque de France, 1960. annual.
Each annual report contains the balance sheets of the different central banks and financial reports on the individual states.

383 **Coton noir, café blanc.** (Black cotton, white coffee.)
Eric de Dampierre. *Cahiers d'Etudes Africaines*, vol. 1 (1960), p. 128-67.
The author emphasizes the disparity between the revenue obtained from the cultivation of cotton by the Africans and the income generated by the European coffee plantations in Ubangi-Shari.

384 **Population et economie de l'Empire Centrafricain.** (The population and economy of the Central African Empire.)
Pierre-Marie Decoudras. *Cahiers d'Outre Mer*, vol. 32, no. 126 (1979), p. 194-204.
Describes the economy of the Central African Empire at the time of the fall of Bokassa.

385 **Le coton.** (Cotton.)
Jean-Louis Duval. Paris: Marcel Didier, 1960. 63p. (Collection 'Mieux Vivre': de la langue à la civilisation française).
This small manual compiled in the last years of colonization was aimed at villagers and coffee planters and was distributed as part of a basic educational campaign to improve the rural environment.

386 **Memento de l'Economie Africaine.** (A summary of the African economy.)
Paris: Ediafric. 1960-85. annual.
Presents a statistical analysis and comments on the various economic and financial sectors of each of the states of French-speaking black Africa.

387 **L'Afrique Noire, Politique et Economique.** (Black Africa, politics and economics.)
Paris: Ediafric, 1960-87. annual.
A country-by-country study which covers general political developments and provides basic statistical data concerning output, budgets, the national debt, credit and foreign aid.

388 **Les plans de développement des pays d'Afrique noire.** (The development plans of the countries of black Africa.)
Paris: Ediafric. 1960-81. annual.
Catalogues the diverse development plans and programmes in the various countries of French-speaking black Africa.

389 **Données et propositions pour engager la préparation du développement.** (Data and proposals designed to encourage the groundwork for development.)
Europrède, Brussels: January-March 1962, 155p.
This study was made in 1961 by a team of experts from the European Planning General Studies and Development Group, which was put at the disposal of the Central African Republic's government by the European Economic Community. Their report defined the main objectives, and laid down the key principles to be followed. Although dated, this report remains topical because of the disappointing results achieved by the Central African Republic during its first thirty years of independence.

390 **Centrafique, riche . . . et pourtant.** (Central Africa, rich . . . but nevertheless.)
Géraldine Faes. *Jeune Afrique Economie*, no. 137 (November 1990), p. 121-25.
Analyses the causes of economic decline in the Central African Republic a failure which was strongly criticized by the opposition in the Central African Republic in a referendum, the results of which were made public in October 1990.

391 **Centrafrique.** (Central Africa.)
Christine Gilguy. *Marchés Tropicaux et Méditeranéens*, no. 2403 (29 November 1991), p. 3067-84.
This special study was carried out by Christine Gilguy, the chief columnist of the weekly *Marchés Tropicaux et Méditeranéens*. After explaining the general state of the economy, the author analyses agriculture and the agro-industry, the mining sector, and finally the secondary and tertiary sectors. However, many of the worrying aspects of the country's present economic situation are not dealt with. It is suggested that with properly directed foreign aid the Central African Republic should be able to survive and escape from economic stagnation.

392 **Les entreprises centrafricaines.** (Central African firms.)
Jean-Pierre Kabylo. *Revue Juridique et Politique, Indépendance et Coopération*, no. 3-4 (July-October 1989), p. 414-25. (XX Congrés à l'IDEF, les Droits de l'homme dans l'Entreprise).
Describes the characteristics of Central African companies.

393 **Réalités Oubanguiennes.** (Ubangian realities.)
Pierre Kalck, foreword by Barthélemy Boganda. Paris: Berger-Levrault, 1959. 356p. maps. bibliog.
This book, awarded a prize by the Académie des Sciences Morales et Politiques in 1961, is an extract from a doctoral thesis presented in 1958, to the Faculty of Law and Economic Sciences in Paris. It recommends a development programme, which was adopted by the Central African government in 1961.

394 **Dossier coton: variations des cours du coton et détérioration des termes de l'échange: le cas de la RCA.** (The cotton issue: variations in the price of cotton and the decline in the exchange rates; the case of the Central African Republic.)
Alain Le Roy. *Marchés Tropicaux* no. 2418 (13 March 1992), p. 679-82.
In 1981, in economic terms, the export of one ton of cotton amounted to the import of nine tons of cement. In 1986, the same export amount was equal to only 3.9 tons of cement. Since then, however, trade has improved to reach an equivalent value of 6.2 tons of cement in 1992.

395 **France-Centrafrique. Ensemble sur le terrain.** (France-Central Africa: together in the field.)
Paris: Ministère de la Coopération, 1990. 72p.
This booklet provides information on Franco-Central African cooperative aid since 1986. It contains notes on the various improvements carried out with French aid in the domains of education; rural development; culture and the arts; telecommunications; agro-industry; research; health; energy and water; the police; customs; the urbanization of transport; as well as computer technology and statistics.

396 **Le code centrafricain des investissements de 1988: mesures et limites de réalisme.** (The central African code of investments of 1988: measures and limits of realism.)
Gabriel Ngouaméné. *Revue Juridique et Politique Indépendance et Coopération* no. 1 (January-March 1991), p. 72-87.
In an attempt to attract capital, the country's authorities established a code for investment that was designed to be advantageous for firms. The author points out that the granting of these advantages also presents some disadvantages.

397 **La situation et la mise en valeur de l'AEF.** (The situation and
exploitation of FEA.)
Paris: La Documentation française, 1951. 66p. (Notes et Etudes
Documentaires no. 1461).
Presents interesting comments on the economic situation of the four territories forming
the federation of French Equatorial Africa in the middle of the twentieth century.

398 **Industrial development review series: Central African Republic.**
ONUDI. Vienna: 1986. 72p. bibliog.
Examines the state of certain industries in central Africa.

399 **Facteurs socio-économiques de l'insuffisance du développement:
l'exemple de la République Centrafricaine.** (Socio-economic factors on
the insuffiiency of development: the example of the Central African
Republic.)
Denis Paye. *Revue Française d'Etudes Politiques Africaines* (April-
May 1985), p. 68-80, p. 97-99. bibliog.
Provides objective analyses, sector by sector, of the economic situation in the Central
Afrian Republic, twenty-five years after independence.

400 **La vie économique de la République Centrafricaine.** (Economic life of
the Central African Republic.)
Jacques Petitjean. Paris: CHEAM, 1966. 205p.
The author, an economic adviser to the French ambassador in Bangui, describes the
economy at the beginning of Bokassa's reign, including the state of foreign firms at the
time.

401 **L'industrie et le commerce en République Centrafricaine.** (Trade and
industry in the Central African Republic.)
Christian Prioul. *Cahiers d'Outre Mer*, no. 88 (October-December
1969), p. 408-29.
This is a good economic study despite the fact that it dates back to 1968. Economic
conditions have deteriorated since then.

402 **Quarterly Economic Review of Gabon, Congo, Cameroon, Central
African Republic, Chad, Equatorial Guinea.**
London: The Economist Intelligence Unit, 1952- . quarterly.
Provides information on the economy in the Central African Republic. This review is
also published annually.

403 **Vues sur l'économie de l'Oubangui-Chari.** (Views about the economy of Ubangi-Shari.)
Jean Romeuf. Paris: Publications économiques et sociales, 1958. 40p.

The author, the secretary-general of the Economic and Social Council in Paris, made this report after a visit to Ubangi-Shari. The document is a good appraisal of the economic situation on the eve of independence.

404 **Le chemin de fer Bangui-Tchad dans son contexte économique régional.**
(The Bangui-Chad railway in its regional economic context.)
Gilles Sauter. Strasbourg, France: Institut de Géographie Appliquée de l'Université de Strasbourg, 1958. 326p.

Although it had been planned since 1913, the construction of a railway linking Bangui to Chad was never realized. The extensive feasibility studies reproduced here were carried out on the very eve of the country's independence.

405 **Rapport sur un projet de liaison ferroviaire Bangui-Fort Lamy.** (A report on a plan for a railway link from Bangui to Fort Lamy.)
Société Civile d'études du Bangui-Tchad, Sofrerail. Paris: Sofrerail, 1959. 123p. map.

On the eve of the Central African Republic's independence, Sofrerail, a branch of the SNCF, examined various studies carried out on the planned railway link between Bangui and Fort Lamy, which has been envisaged since 1913. The expert authors of this report give their opinions on the possibility of constructing this railway, and consider both the investment needed and the technical feasibility of the project. Three years later the plan was abandoned.

406 **Une économie sous perfusion.** (An economy under cover.)
Laurent Zecchini. *Le Monde*, (30 November 1984), p. 13-14.

The author stresses the importance of French aid to the Central African Republic. France has had to increase its donations to the Central African Republic considerably since 1979, due to a serious deterioration of the CAR's economy. Economic development remains markedly handicapped because of the enclosed location of the country, and since independence, no remedy to the situation has been found.

La République Centrafricaine. (The Central African Republic.)
See item no. no. 2.

Atlas de la République Centrafricaine. (Atlas of the Central African Republic.)
See item no. 9.

Histoire de la centrafrique, violence du développement, domination et inégalités. (History of Central Africa, the violence of development, domination and inequality.)
See item no. 218.

Agriculture, Forests and Animal Husbandry

407 **Le café en Oubangui-Chari.** (Coffee in Ubangi-Shari.)
Anon. *Marchés Tropicaux*, (15 March 1958), p. 701-04.
Provides a history of coffee cultivation in Ubangi-Shari, and discusses both the total destruction of the excelsa coffee plantations between 1936 and 1945 due to trachiomycosis, as well as the dramatic increase in robusta coffee plantations between 1950 and 1954.

408 **L'approvisionnement en poisson de la ville de Bangui.** (Supplying fish to the town of Bangui.)
Jean-Marie Bassangui. MA thesis, Université de Bordeaux III, 1988. 359p.
Bassangui describes the factors governing the production, marketing and consumption of fish in Bangui. All fish has to be imported since none is available locally.

409 **Cultures alimentaires de la région du Gribingui.** (Food cultivation in the Gribingui region.)
A. Baudon. Marseille: Annales Musée Colonial, 1913. 32p. (Third Series).
Considers subsistence cultivation practised by the Ubangians at the beginning of the colonial period.

410 **Expertise sur le développement de la région centre-sud.** (An expert evaluation of development in the central-south region.)
A. Benitès. Paris: BDPA, 1986. 105p.
The economic importance of the region studied is substantial. Seventy-two per cent of the country's production is carried out on twenty-one per cent of its surface area.

Agriculture, Forests and Animal Husbandry

411 **Production et commercialisation du bétail et de la viande en RCA.** (The production and marketing of livestock and meat in the CAR.)
J. Berkoula. Paris; Maisons-Alfort, France: Université de Paris XII, IEMVT, 1983. 100p.

Tables of production and marketing, region by region, together with annotations are provided in this volume.

412 **L'élevage bovin en République Centrafricaine.** (Cattle breeding in the Central African Republic.)
Philippe Bertucat. Maisons-Alfort, France: Imprimerie Au manuscrit, 1965. 101p.

A consideration of animal husbandry in the first years of independence, by a veterinary surgeon attached to the Siège de l'Ecole Nationale Vétérinaire and to the IEMVT (Institut d'Elevage et de Médecine Vétérinaire Tropicale).

413 **Des Peuls en savanes humides. Développement pastoral dans l'Ouest Centrafricain.** (The Foulbé in humid savannas: pastoral development in the west of central Africa.)
Jean Boutrais. Paris: Editions de l'ORSTOM, 1988. 391p.

Provides an in-depth study of pastoral activity in the Bouar-Baboua region. Breeder's needs and resources, outside help, and a development and breeding plan in this particularly favourable region are all described. The author stresses the importance of professional training and the organization of the profession of animal breeding. Known for his earlier work on animal husbandry in Cameroon, Philippe Boutrais is one of the few researchers to actually speak the Fulfuldé language of the Mbororo animal breeders.

414 **Le problème de la viande en Oubangui-Chari. Son évolution. Son importance économique et sociale.** (The meat problem in Ubangi-Shari: its evolution and economic and social importance.)
Henri Brizard. *Revue d'Elevage et de Médecine Vétérinaire des Pays Tropicaux*, vol. 6, no. 1 (January-March 1953), p. 9-15.

Presents a history of the introduction from Cameroon, from 1924 onwards, of domestic cattle in the northwest of Ubangi-Shari, and describes the creation in 1938, of a new breeding zone in the Bambari region, right in the centre of the territory. The author, the head of veterinary services in the former colony, underlines the importance of a herd that numbered more than 350,000 in 1951, in providing the population with food.

415 **Staff appraisal report. Central African Empire. Livestock development project.**
R. Brown, Yves Cheneau. Washington, DC. Banque Mondiale, 1978. 53p.

This document was submitted to the World Bank.

416   **Relance du ranch de la Mbali (Empire Centrafricain).** (The revival of
        the Mbali ranch [Central African Empire].)
        Paul Capitaine, G. Gouet.   Maisons-Alfort, France: IEMVT, 1977.
        168p.
Reports on a ranching improvement and development project in the northwest of the
country.

417   **Le parasitisme des cultures cotonnières en République Centrafricaine:
        définition des moyens de lutte.** (The incidence of cotton pests in the
        Central African Republic: a definition of pest control.)
        J. Cauquil, B. Girardot, P. Vincent.   *Coton et Fibres Tropicales*,
        vol. 41, no. 1 (1986), p. 5-19. map.
French agronomists carried out important research to combat the high incidence of
cotton pests in central Africa's cotton fields.

418   **Projet de développement rural intégré des savanes du nord-est de la
        République Centrafricaine.** (Integrated rural development project in
        the savannas of the northeast of the Central African Republic.)
        J. Coulomb.   Paris: GERDAT, 1978. 90p.
Rural development in the eastern region of the Central African Republic has
encountered enormous difficulties because the area is so sparsely populated. There are
not even enough inhabitants to maintain the tracks which run across the region.

419   **La lutte contre les glossines dans le zone d'action pastorale de Yeremo
        (République Centrafricaine).** (Tsetse fly control in the pastoral land
        action area of Yeremo, Central African Republic.)
        Dominique Cuisance.   Maisons-Alfort, France: IEMVT, 1988. 68p.
        3 maps.
This report points out the extent of the trypanosomiasis in the area concerned, which
consists of 700 kilometres of gallery forests. The author recommends the use of traps at
the watering holes, and by the cattle breeders themselves.

420   **Plantes alimentaires du pays banda.** (Food plants in the Banda region.)
        R. P. Joseph Daigre.   *Bulletin de la Société des Recherches Congolaises*,
        no. 8, variétés III, 1927, p. 126-34.
The author points out that at this time (ca. 1927) the diverse traditional food plants
cultivated in the hut gardens ensured that the villagers had a varied diet. The numbers
of such gardens have subsequently decreased and have led to the disappearance of
some of the plants. Agronomists hope that the plants can be re-introduced by the re-
cultivation of the gardens which have been abandoned.

Agriculture, Forests and Animal Husbandry

421 **Situation actuelle de l'élevage en République Centrafricaine.** (Animal husbandry today in the Central African Republic.)
Jean Desrotour. Maisons-Alfort, France: IEMVT, 1981. 67p
The author, a veterinary surgeon, devoted his entire career to the development of animal breeding in Central Africa. As this account reveals, his career was examplary.

422 **Les bovins trypanotolérants; leur élevage en République Centrafricaine.** (Trypanotolerant cattle: breeding them in the Central African Republic.)
Jean Desrotour, Pierre Finelle, Paul Martin, Eugène Sinodinos. *Revue d'Elevage et de Médecine Vétérinaire des Pays Tropicaux*, vol. 10, (New series no. 4 (1967), p. 589-94.
Between 1956 and 1967 about 4,000 Baoule sires were imported to Central Africa and kept in a métayage system (the system whereby the farmer pays rent in kind, the land owner furnishing the stock) in trypanosomiasis-infected areas. Unfortunately, after the departure of Dr Desrotour, the system broke down and the experiment failed.

423 **Projet de réhabilitation des plantations industrielles de caféiers.** (A rehabilitation project in the industrial coffee tree plantations.)
Jacques Deuss. Paris: IFCC, 1986. 335p. 3 vols.
The programme suggested here advocates the regeneration of coffee trees by pruning, the use of insecticides, the replanting of coffee trees destroyed by fire and the extension of plantations to previously cleared land.

424 **L'apiculture en Empire Centrafricain. Situation et perspectives.** (Bee-keeping in the Central African Empire: the present situation and the prospects for the future.)
M. Douhet. Maisons-Alfort, France: IEMVT, 1979. 70p. maps.
Wild honey was marketed throughout the colonial period. It formed an extra resource for the villagers in the east. This article is valuable because it outlines and discusses a simple programme designed to develop bee-keeping and to provide income.

425 **La caféiculture en Oubangui-Chari.** (Coffee cultivation in Ubangi-Shari.)
René Drouillon. Bangui: Service de l'Agriculture de l'AEF, imprimerie centrale d'Afrique Brazzaville, 1957. 223p. bibliog.
In the 1950s, the European coffee planters were hostile to the development of family plantations in the villages. Notwithstanding this, the technicians from the agriculture service, including the author, encouraged the villagers. The first part of this work, written intentionally for the planters, gives the basic techniques and practices of coffee cultivation in Ubangi-Shari (p. 1-152). The second part is devoted to the diseases and parasites of the coffee trees in Ubangi (p. 153-222).

426   **Le colatier en République Centrafricaine.** (The cola tree in the Central African Republic.)
Pierre Dublin. *Café, Cacao, Thé*, vol. 9, no. 2, (April-June 1965), p. 97-115; vol. 9, no. 3, (July-September 1965), p. 175-92.

Four years of study have enabled the author, at the Boukoko station (Lobaye), to select heads of clones (i.e., cuttings) and to find out the cultivation requirements of the cola tree. He recommends that combined plantations of coffee trees and cola trees could be economically worthwhile.

427   **Le caféier excelsa en République centrafricaine.** (The excelsa coffee tree in the Central African Republic.)
Pierre Dublin. *Café, Cacao, Thé*, vol. 5, no. 1, (January-March 1961), p. 11-27; vol. 7, no. 1, p. 6-21.

Dublin provides general data about the new possibilities for excelsa coffee tree cultivation in the Central African Republic. The author believes that the central African excelsa coffee trees could be economically viable in the production of instant coffee.

428   **Les possibilités d'accroissement de la production cotonnière en AEF (Oubangui-Tchad).** (The possibilities for increasing cotton production in FEA – Ubangi-Chad.)
René Dumont. Paris: Institut Agronomique, 1950. 125p.

During a mission to Ubangi and Chad in 1949, the engineer, René Dumont, recommended a concentration of cotton cultivation in the most favourable areas.

429   **Le difficile développement agricole de la République Centrafricaine.** (The difficult agricultural development of the Central African Republic.)
René Dumont. *Annales de l'Institut National Agronomique*, 1966. 85p.

At the end of an investigative assignment requested by the Central African Republic government, the author drew up a critical analysis of the country's agricultural situation. He recommends drastic measures to improve it.

430   **Les possibilités de la culture de la roselle (hibiscus sabdariffa) et du kenaf (hibiscus cannabinus) en RCA.** (The feasibility of growing roselle and kenaf in the Central African Republic.)
Jean-Claude Follin, A. Fritz. *Coton et Fibres Tropicales*, 19, vol. 23, no. 3, (1968), p. 375-82.

Alleges that the domestic production of roselle fibre would make it possible to avoid having to import jute for the packaging of coffee and cotton intended for export.

431   **Culture du caféier robusta en Afrique Centrale.** (Robusta coffee cultivation in central Africa.)
Jean Forestier. Paris: IFCC, 1969. 206p.

This basic work consists of three parts covering: firstly, the robusta coffee tree and its requirements, the preparation of the land, plantations and their upkeep, the cultivation of the plants, harvesting and manufacture; secondly, the training of the work-force, organizational and working methods in the small and family plantations; and thirdly, the value of the plantations, prices, coffee sales, and the economic viability of the family plantations.

432   **Agroclimatologie du Centrafrique.** (Agroclimatology in central Africa.)
Pierre Franquin, Roland Diziain, Jean-Paul Cointepas, Yves
Boulvert.   Paris: ORSTOM, 1988. 522p.

Describes the three types of climate found in the Central African Republic: Guinean-forest; Sudano-Guinean; and Sahelo-Guinean. The distribution of the vegetation reflects the climatic differences; dense forest in the south, scrub land in the centre, and open savanna in the north. The Central African soils conceal large hydric reserves, which are often under-estimated. The data used here comes from ninety-five stations spread throughout the territory.

433   **L'évolution de l'agriculture autochtone dans les savanes de l'Oubangui-Chari.** (The development of autochthonous agriculture in the savannas of Ubangi-Shari.)
René Guillemin.   *L'Agronomie Tropicale*, vol. 11, no. 1
(January-February 1956), p. 39-61; no. 2 (March-April 1956),
p. 143-76; no. 3 (May-June 1956), p. 279-309.

This study carried out by the General Inspector of Agriculture in the FEA completes the work started by Father Tisserant (q.v.). His work is essential to anyone interested in the agricultural development of the central African savannas.

434   **Wildlife research in Manova-Gounda-Saint Floris National Park.**
H.B. Hulberg, Richard W. Carrol.   Washington, DC: US Peace Corps,
1982. 345p. maps.

Discusses studies of the fauna to be found in the nature reserves of central Africa.

435   **Boeufs et vaches à Agoudou-Manga.** (Oxen and cows at Agoudou-Manga.)
R.P. Jean Hyernard.   Abidjan, Ivory Coast: INADES, 1966. 127p.

Describes experiments, pioneered by the Catholic missionaries, in the use of animals for draught in the Banda region.

436   **La mécanisation de l'agriculture en République Centrafricaine.** (The mechanization of agriculture in the Central African Republic.)
C. Jannaud, J. Kellerman.   Bangui: Ministry of Development, 1967.
320p.

The introduction of mechanized agricultural methods in central Africa was fraught with difficulties, as detailed here.

437 **Manual of forest botany. Tropical Africa.**
René Letouzey, translated from the French by R. Mugget,
R. Harrison. Nogent-sur-Marne, France: Centre Technique Forestier
Tropicale, 1986. 2 vols.
Volume 1 (204p.) deals in a general way, despite the title of the book, with trees,
shrubs and herbaceous plants. It also outlines the various species to be found in
tropical Africa and provides a great number of practical details concerning collecting
and conserving botany samples. Volumes 2a and 2b (230p.) deal with successive
families of plants (trees, shrubs and herbaceous plants) represented in dense, moist or
dry forests as well as in savanna and steppes.

438 **Le café dans la colonie française de l'Oubangui-Chari.** (Coffee in the
French colony of Ubangi-Shari.)
Jean L'Huillier. Paris: Imprimerie Humbert, 1933. 63p.
The author recommends excelsa coffee trees because of their resistance to fire. He did
not foresee, however, the tracheo-mycosis disease that was to wipe out all of the
central African excelsa coffee plantations, within a few years.

439 **L'exploitation de la cire en AEF.** (The exploitation of wax in FEA.)
René Malbrant. Brazzaville: Imprimerie du gouvernement général,
1941. 9p.
There were numerous wax markets in Ubangi-Shari, especially in the east and the sales
of this product brought considerable extra income to the peoples of central Africa.

440 **Manuel de l'éleveur et du moniteur d'élevage. (Moyen-Congo, Gabon et
Sud de l'Oubangui.)** (The animal breeder and breeding monitor's
manual: Moyen-Congo, Congo and South of Ubangi.)
René Malbrant. Brazzaville: Imprimerie du gouvernement général,
1955. 143p.
This manual represents the first attempt at providing a basic education in animal
breeding in countries which, at that time, had only just begun to breed stock.

441 **La valorisation des sous-produits du coton en République
Centrafricaine.** (The development of cotton by-products in the Central
African Republic.)
Michel Maumon, Yves Bagot, Justin Gutknecht. Paris: Office of the
Secretary of State in relations with the States of the Community, 1960.
64p.
Shows that, after ginning the cotton, a considerable number of by-products can be
produced at little cost, producing considerable extra income for the planters.

442 **Contribution à l'étude des systèmes de production traditionnelle en pays Dakpa (région de Grimari).** (A contribution to the study of the systems of traditional agricultural production in Dakpa country – Grimari region.)
G. Meurillon. *Coton et Fibres Tropicaux*, vol. 36, part 2 (1981), p. 137-54. map.

The author presents an overall approach to the system of production in a region of the Central African savanna. He places this in the more general context of the daily constraints of the traditional way of life, showing the aims, methods and results of the traditional agricultural practices.

443 **Le coton en Afrique de l'ouest et du centre: situation et perspectives.** (Cotton in western and central Africa: the present situation and the prospects for the future.)
Ministère de la coopération. Paris: CCCE, CIRAP, SEDES, CFDT, 1987. 233p. 13 maps.

Presents and analyses some of the existing data on cotton production in nine countries of French-speaking Africa, including the Central African Republic. The nine countries produce only two per cent of the world's total output, but 7.4 per cent of the world's cotton exports. Cotton production in Central Africa is the most precarious and suffers because of the enclosed location of the country. The product is, however, of good quality and is used in the manufacture of velvet.

444 **Etude pour une stratégie alimentaire.** (A study designed to formulate a food strategy.)
Y. Ouault, Y. Darricau. Paris: BDPA, 1985. 146p.

The aim of this study was to evaluate the food and nutritional situation of the Central African Republic at this time (mid-1980s), to forecast the long-term picture (2010) and to suggest a possible strategy.

445 **Situation actuelle de l'élevage de bovins trypano-résistants en Empire Centrafricain.** (The current situation of trypano-resistant cattle breeding in the Central African Empire.)
Henri Peletan. Maisons-Alfort, France: IEMVT, 1979. 79p.

The breeding of trypano-resistant cattle is linked to the problematic introduction of methods of cultivation involving draught animals in the Central African Republic.

446 **Etude phyto-écologique et cartographique de Parc National Manovo-Gounda-Saint Floris (République Centrafricaine).** (A phyto-ecological and cartographical study of the Manovo-Gounda-Saint Floris National Park, the Central African Republic.)
Bernard Peyre de Fabrègues, Gordano Forgiarini, Gérald de Wispelaire (et al.). Maisons-Alfort, France: IEMVT, 1981. 146p. maps.

This is an important contribution to the study of Central Africa's most beautiful natural park. The park's fauna is seriously threatened by poaching.

447 **Les défrichements culturaux et la savanisation de l'Oubangui-Chari.**
(The land cleared for cultivation and the spread of the savanna in
Ubangi-Shari.)
Roger Sillans. *Agronomie Tropicale* 7 (1955), p. 431-36.

Following an expedition to Ubangi-Shari in 1950, in the company of Professor August
Chevalier, Roger Sillans was able to assess the exact influence of the clearing of the
land for cultivation and the persistence of a rich dense forest in the unpopulated east of
the country.

448 **Application de la recherche à la mise en valeur des ressources
cynégétiques.** (The application of research for the development of
cynegetic resources.)
J.P. Thomassey. Nogent-sur-Marne, France: CTFT, 1981. 83p.

Asserts that a considerable amount of research is necessary to protect the country's
fauna.

449 **L'agriculture dans les savanes de l'Oubangui.** (Agriculture in the
savannas of Ubangi.)
R.P. Charles Tisserant. *Bulletin de l'Institut d'Etudes Centrafricaines*
6 (1953), p. 209-73.

The author, a missionary, ethnologist and distinguished botanist, deplores the
destruction of the vast plantations that he knew when he arrived in Ubangi at the
beginning of the century. He regrets the very marked decrease in the number of
cultivated species and reminds the reader that the traditional cultivation techniques
were passed down from generation to generation during the initiation of the young.

450 **L'économie forestière dans le sud-ouest de la République Centrafricaine.**
(The forest economy in the southwest of the Central African Republic.)
P. Yalimendet. Bordeaux: MA thesis, Université de Bordeaux,
France. 1986. 315p.

The author studied the main consequences of forest exploitation on the traditional
social structures.

Atlas de la République Centrafricaine. (Atlas of the Central African
Republic.)
See item no. 9.

Enquête agricole en RCA, 1960-1961. (Agricultural survey in CAR, 1960-
1961.)
See item no. 293.

La vie rurale chez les Banda. (Rural life of the Banda.)
See item no. 305.

Alimentation, approvisionnement et agriculture in Bangui.)
See item no. 338.

Agriculture, Forests and Animal Husbandry

Ville et agriculture rivière en RCA. (Town and river agriculture in the CAR.)
See item no. 339.

Production cotonnière et développement. (Cotton production and development.)
See item no. 380.

Le coton. (Cotton.)
See item no. 385.

Education

451 **Eveil à la vie centrafricaine.** (Waking up to life in central Africa.)
Marie-France Adrien-Rongier. Bangui: UNICEF, Ministère des
Affaires Sociales, 1979. 64p.
This is a useful guide to every-day life in Central Africa and is aimed at children
engaged in primary education.

452 **L'éducation sexuelle en milieu scolaire ou préparation à la vie familiale.**
(Sex education at school or preparation for family life.)
M. Crabbe, C. Farra-Frond. Bangui: Ministère de la Santé, 1985.
110p.
Presents advice on sex education for use by teachers in schools in the Central African
Republic.

453 **Rapport sur l'expérience d'éducation de base en Oubangui-Chari.**
(Report about the experiment of basic education in Ubangi-Shari.)
Pierre Fourré. Paris: Centre National de Documentation
Pédagogique, 1952. 76p.
Carried out on the initiative of the Governor-General of FEA, this pilot operation was
designed to prepare the way for the establishment of a basic literary and education
programme for people of all ages but especially adults. It was set up at the village level
in the centre of Ubangi-Shari. David Dacko, a young primary school teacher,
participated in this scheme.

454 **Les langues de l'Empire Centrafricain et l'enseignement des mathématiques.** (The languages of the Central African Empire and the teaching of mathematics.)
H. Magdalena. *Annales de l'Université J.B. Bokassa*, vol. II (1977), p. 362-75.

Discusses the use of common and vernacular languages in order to achieve improvements in the teaching of mathematics.

455 **Les randonnées de Daba (de Ouadda à Bangui).** (Daba's travels, from Ouadda to Bangui.)
Pierre Bamboté. Paris: Éditions La Farandole 1966, 160p; New York: Pantheon Books, 1971.

This highly pedagogical story recounts the itinerary of a child going from Upper Kotto to Bangui to study. It provides a very good analysis of the feelings he experiences at this important stage in his life.

456 **Manuel d'hygiène scolaire.** (A school handbook of hygiene.)
Anne-Marie Pereira. Bangui: Institut pédagogique national, 1980. 190p.

Presents ways in which children can be taught better methods of hygiene thus improving health standards in Central Africa.

Literature, Memoirs and Folklore

457 **Les deux oiseaux de l'Ubangi.** (The two birds of Ubangi.)
Makambo Bamboté. Paris: Editions St. Germain des Prés, 1968. 76p.
Describes how two central African children discover the life, customs and wider characteristics of their community. The same author also wrote *Les randonnées de Daba* (q.v.).

458 **Princesse Mandapu.** (Princess Mandapu.)
Makambo Bamboté. Paris: Présence Africaine, 1972. 187p.
Provides scenes of daily life in a family of state employees in the Central African Republic.

459 **Nouvelles de Bangui.** (News of Bangui.)
Makambo Bamboté. Montreal: Les Presses de l'Université de Montréal, 1980. 167p.
These fourteen pieces of news written in 1963 and 1964 earned their author, a former Director of Information in Bangui who sought refuge in Canada in 1973 and now lives there with his family, an award from the revue *Études françaises*. This revue was first established in 1966 by the publishing firm of Thérien Brothers. This volume contains an account of the death of Chief Sayo, the son of Bangassou, the king of the Nzakara, and one of the author's relatives.

460 **Coup d'Etat nègre.** (A negroe coup d'etat.)
Makambo Bamboté. Montréal: Humanitas, 1987. 117p.
The author, the former director of information at Bangui at the time of the Saint Sylvestré coup d'état, describes with much realism the scenes he witnessed on the night of 31 December/1 January 1966. No other Central African Republic citizen has risked describing this tragic night when President David Dacko was forced to flee the town as a result of this coup. The Commander of the Gendarmes, Jean-Henri Izamo, was

ready to take power but was lured into an ambush by the Chief of Staff, Jean-Bedel Bokassa, and assassinated..

461 **Journey to the end of the night.** (Voyage au bout de la nuit.)
Louis-Ferdinand Céline, translated from the French by Ralph Manheim. London: John Calder, 1988. Originally published as *Voyage au bout de la Nuit*, Paris: Gallimard 1932. New edition annotated by Henri Godard, 1981. 159p.

Céline devotes more than sixty pages to Equatorial Africa at the beginning of the century, using his memories of his time as an agent of the Sangha-Ubangi Forestry Company.

462 **Lettres et premiers écrits d'Afrique 1916-1917.** (Letters and early writings of Africa 1916-1917.)
Louis-Ferdinand Céline, texts assembled and presented by Jean-Pierre Dauphin. Paris: NRF Gallimard, Cahiers Céline no. 4, 1978. 207p.

The eighty-two letters and postcards, two poems, twenty lines of translation and one short story reproduced here make it possible to reconstuct the author's [Louis Destouches] African itinerary in 1916 and 1917. Louis Destouches, at that time aged twenty-two, was in the Sangha-Ubangi Forestry Company. He was put in charge of a factory, then of a plantation of this concessionary company in Cameroon, which had recently been conquered by the French.

463 **L'imperatore.** (The Emperor.)
Maurizio Chierici. Milan, Italy: Rizzoli Editore, 1980. 229p.

The author recounts the incredible story of the Emperor Bokassa I. He pays particular attention to the relationship between President Valéry Giscard d'Estaing and the Central African Republic's despot.

464 **L'Etat sauvage.** (The wild State.)
Georges Conchon. Paris: Albin Michel, 1964. 267p. (Prix Goncourt).

Drawing on his experiences as Secretary-General of the Central African National Assembly for several months in 1960-61, the author has produced a novel in which the reader has absolutely no trouble in recognizing the places and personalities of Bangui, which is called Fort-Jacul in the book.

465 **Un soleil au bout de la nuit.** (Light at the end of the tunnel.)
Gabriel Danzi. Dakar, Abidjan, Lomé: Nouvelles Editions Africaines, 1985. 254p.

The chronicle of a Mbomu village in which the author criticizes the rural exodus towards Bangui. Danzi shows how life in the capital is breaking down all the traditional values.

466 **La manipulation.** (Manipulation.)
Roger Delpey. Paris: J. Grancher, 1981. 346p.

The author, a former French non-commissioned officer in the Indochina war, went into Bokassa's service just before his fall from power. Arrested in Paris on the 11 May 1980 as he was leaving the Libyan Embassy, Delpey was sentenced to six months in Santé Prison. President Valéry Giscard d'Estaing believed that he possessed correspondence that might compromise him. This book is both a real attempt to clear the name of the Central African tyrant and to settle scores with the President of the French Republic, on the eve of the presidential elections. The last eighty-six pages reproduce the inter-African observation mission's report, annotated by the author, that was sent to Bangui in June 1979, implicating Bokassa in genocide.

467 **Prisonnier de Giscard.** (Giscard's prisoner.)
Roger Delpey. Paris: Jacques Grancher, 1982. 353p.

The author recounts the 222 days he spent in the Santé Prison in Paris and discusses his relationship with Bokassa. He also presents a sharp diatribe against the President of the French Republic and his Central African policies.

468 **Affaires centrafricaines. Quand le Centrafrique bougera, l'Afrique explosera.** (Central African Affairs: when Central Africa stirs, Africa will explode.)
Roger Delpey. Paris: Jacques Grancher, 1985. 248p.

This pamphlet represents a vitriolic condemnation of General André Kolingba's government and its relationship with France.

469 **Le blanc et le noir, le hold-up du siècle.** (The white man and the black man, the hold-up of the century.)
Roger Delpey. Paris: Jacques Grancher, 1991. 242p.

The author brings together some eye-witness accounts describing the removal of archives and various objects belonging to Emperor Bokassa by French parachutists in September 1979. In addition, he describes what became known as the 'Giscard's diamonds affair' when the French press revealed that Valéry Giscard d'Estaing had retained diamonds given to him by the Emperor.

470 **La crotte tenace et autres contes n'gbaka-ma'bo de la République Centrafricaine.** (Persistent rubbish and other N'gbaka-Ma'bo tales from the Central African Republic.)
Marie-José Dérivé, Jacqueline Thomas, Marcel Madove. Paris: SELAF, 1975. 227p. (Langues et Civilisations à Tradition Orale no. 13).

Presents nine tales in vernacular language (phonetic transcription), with their French translation.

471 **La rivière de guerre, roman.** (The river of war, novel.)
Michel Droit. Paris: Julliard, 1985. 321p.

A member of the *Académie Française*, Michel Droit was also a hunting guide in Central Africa. He tells the story, in novel form, of the adventures in the Central African bush of two former French soldiers. The soldiers are veterans of the colonial wars of Indochina, Algeria and Katanga and relive their memories of war.

Literature, Memoirs and Folklore

472   **L'empereur.** (The Emperor.)
      Jacques Duchemin. Paris: Albin Michel, 1981. 363p.

The author, who was Tschombé's Minister of War and then Tombalbaye's political adviser, became a minister in Bokassa's imperial court just before his downfall. This story about a psychotic character, contains disturbing features. In fact, a journalist from *Le Monde* wrote that it was 'a book by a madman about a madman'.

473   **L'Afrique.** (Africa.)
      Valéry Giscard d'Estaing.   In: *Le pouvoir et la vie, II l'affrontement.*
      Paris: Editions Compagnie 12, 1991, p. 274-356.

Bewitched by the country, President Giscard d'Estaing carried out a series of trips to the Central African Republic, several of which were devoted to hunting. He recalls the events that led him to order French soldiers to put an end to Emperor Bokassa's regime in 1979. Some explanations about the so-called diamond affair, which definitely played a role in his electoral defeat of 1981, are included.

474   **Sangba Turé (Zande folklore.)**
      E.C. Gore.   London: Sheldon Press, 1931. 116p.

The author presents the cunning hero, Turé or Tulé, about whom the Central African villagers, and notably the Zande, like to make the subject of adventure stories.

475   **Quelques récits du Centrafrique: une contribution à l'oralité.** (Some stories from central Africa: a contribution to folklore.)
      Joachim Guélemby. Paris, 1987. 85p.

The author was an English teacher in Bangui, and at the time this book was written was the Central African Republic's ambassador to UNESCO. In his tales he evokes the mythical character of Tulé the rogue, and of Bandimbakolo, the oldest lady. His works reveal the profound wisdom that inspires the Nzakara-Zande culture.

476   **Le silence de la forêt.** (The silence of the forest.)
      Etienne Goyemidé. Paris: Hatier, 1984. 160p.

The story of a man who gives up everything to go in search of the pygmies of the 'Great Forest'. The civilization and daily life of the pygmies living in the forests of the Sangha (CAR and Congo) are the subject of two important recent studies: Noël Ballif's *Les pygmées de la Grande Forêt* (The pygmies of the Great Forest) Paris: L'Harmattan 1992, 240p. (Connaissance des hommes); and Louis Sarno's *Song from the forest: My life among the Ba-Benjellé Pygmies* London: Bantam, 1993, 288p.

477   **Le dernier survivant de la caravane.** (The last survivor of the caravans.)
      Etienne Goyemidé. Paris: Hatier, 1985. 127p.

This novel recounts the tragedy that took place until the beginning of the twentieth century, namely the hunt for slaves, which was practised in the north, the east and the centre of Ubangi. Goyemidé also describes the transport of the slaves, by caravans, to the slave markets in Muslim countries.

478 **Le lac des sorciers.** (The lake of sorcerors.)
Faustin-Albert Ipeko-Etomane. Yaoundé: Editions Clé, collection pour tous, 1972. 46p.

This Central African state servant, originally from Ippy in the Banda region, presents four short stories inspired by traditional legends, or scenes of present-day village life in this region.

479 **Tous n'étaient pas des anges.** (Not everyone was an angel.)
Joseph Kessel. Paris: Plon, 1963. 290p.

In this work, the author, a former officer in the Free French Air Force and a member of the Académie Française, brings together seventeen heroic accounts from the Second World War. In the chapter entitled 'Le fusillé' ('The shot man', p. 237-59), he recounts the adventure of Captain Conus, a coffee planter and animal hunter, who was one of the first Frenchmen from Ubangi to join up with General de Gaulle. After parachuting into the Vercors, and being captured by the Germans, Conus managed to escape just as he was about to be executed.

480 **Terre d'Ebène, la traite des noirs.** (Earth of ebony, the black slave trade.)
Albert Londres. Paris: Albin Michel, 1929. 268p.

This French journalist, who died in 1932, and who believed his job was to 'put the pen in the wound', stirred up opinion against the Cayenne penal colony, Africa's disciplinary battalions, psychiatric asylums and brothels. In this book, he denounces the scandal of the Congo-Ocean railway line construction site, where thousands of Central Africans, notably Sara, Banda and Gbaya, perished.

481 **Batouala, roman nègre.** (Batouala, a negro novel.)
René Maran. Paris: Albin Michel, 1921. 190p.

Presents the story of Chief Batouala in the Banda region and recounts the daily life of the Ubangian villagers during colonization. The author, a former subdivision head in Ubangi and a friend of Eboué, was the object of vicious attacks by the colonizers, who strongly disliked and resented his account. René Maran received the Prix Goncourt for this book.

482 **Djouma, chien de brousse.** (Djouma, bush dog.)
René Maran. Paris: Albin Michel, 1927. 253p.

This book complements the famous novel *Batouala*. Old chief Batouala's dog was a 'good sort', who 'was never given anything' and 'never asked for anything'. Through Djouma, the whole wretched daily life of a village in Banda country is told in a gripping way.

483 **Légendes et contes nègres de l'Oubangui-Chari.** (Negro legends and tales from Ubangi-Shari.)
René Maran. Paris: Albin Michel and Les Oeuvres libres, 1933. 122p.

A collection of legends by the author of 'Batouala'.

484 **Léon la France.** (Léon, France.)
Léon Mercier. Paris: Private Archives, Actes Sud, Hubert Nyssen, 1989. 211p.

Philippe Mercier's grandfather, a sergeant in the colonial infantry, arrived in Bangui on 4 September 1901, in order to take part in the battles for the conquest of Chad. The letters that he wrote to his family form a good witness account of this period.

485 **Wanto, the hero of Gbaya tradition.**
Philip A. Noss. *Journal of the Folklore Institute*, vol. 8, no. 1 (1971), p. 3-16.

The author, an expert on the Gbaya people, brings together the traditions concerning this legendary hero, about whom little it known. Wanto, the 'civilizing hero', teaches the men tales and fables, each one revealing a social or moral rule.

486 **Littérature centrafricaine.** (Central African literature.)
Office du Livre. Cercle des Lecteurs d'expression française (Clef).
Afrique, Océan Indien, Notre libraire, no. spécial 1989. 132p.

This is a collection of works chosen from the writings of contemporary Central African writers.

487 **Cours de littérature orale centrafricaine. Recueil de textes.** (A course in central African oral literature: a collection of texts.)
Jean-Dominique Penel. Bangui: Faculté des Lettres et des Sciences Humaines, 1980-83. 2 vols.

Oral literature occupies an important place in the traditional culture of central Africa as revealed in these texts.

488 **Anthologie de la poésie centrafricaine.** (An anthology of central African poetry.)
Jean-Dominique Penel. Paris: L'Harmattan, 1990. 208p.

This anthology contains examples of the best current poetry and contains an introduction by a French teacher, who, despite the fact that initially she had no knowledge of the subject, was given the task of teaching central African literature.

489 **Poètes Nzakara.** (Nzakara poets.)
Edited by Eric de Dampierre. Paris: Editions Julliard, 1953. 222p.
(Classique Africans).

The texts assembled and translated by Eric de Dampierre are the first texts written in the Nzakara language to be published. With the help of Robert Bangbanzi, Dampierre has selected tales that enable a better understanding of the 'mind' of this population, and the role of the poet in society (p. 13-33). Notes are provided about the Nzakara language (p. 35-39).

490 **Terre de soleil et de sommeil.** (Land of sun and sleep.)
     Ernest Psichari. Paris: Louis Conard, 1933. 264p.

Sergeant Ernest Psichari, Ernest Renan's grandson, accompanied Commander Lenfant on his mission to west central Africa and the Logone in 1906-07. In his preface, the author himself presents 'these essays, whose aim is only to give some aspects of African life'. He adds: 'Their only worth is that they were written with love. Africa has its faithful. This land makes us better people. It excites us and lifts us above ourselves, into a tension where dream and action penetrate'. The Gbaya region particularly has inspired this great French poet.

491 **Contes du pays Nzakara.** (Tales from the Nzakara region.)
     Anne Retel-Laurentin. Paris: Karthala, 1986. 310p.

The author publishes tales recorded from forty-four Nzakara story-tellers, then translated into French. These texts provide a better understanding of the material life, social heirarchy and family worries of the Nzakara population.

492 **L'odyssée de Mongou.** (The Mongou odyssey.)
     Pierre Sammy-Macfoy. Paris: Hatier, 1983. 127p. (Collection Monde
     Noir en Poche).

Recounts the adventures of Mongou, a Bandia village chief mobilized in the army in the Second World War. Mongou suddenly discovers the world beyond his village, then goes to France.

493 **Le colonisateur colonisé.** (The colonizer colonized.)
     Louis Sanmarco. Paris: Editions Pierre-Marcel Favre, ABC, l'Afrique
     en marche, 1983. 229p.

This autobiography reads like a novel. The author has twice served in Central Africa: first as a student-administrator of the colonies in 1936 at Ngotto (Boda district in the Lobaye region), then as Governor and head of the territory of Ubangi-Shari from 1953 to 1957. The account of these two periods in Louis Sanmarco's career make up the best pages of this book of memoirs, which is also a justification of his work as an administrator. In this work the author also recalls his privileged relationship, and then split, with Barthélemy Boganda.

494 **Le diamant noir. Comment on devient ambassadeur d'Israel.** (The black
     diamond: how to become ambassador of Israel.)
     Ovadia Soffer. Paris: Robert Laffont, 1987. 285p.

The author, who is the Israeli ambassador to France, relates his diplomatic career. He devotes 131 pages to his stay in Bangui from 1963 to 1967, as first adviser at the Israeli embassy. He evokes his friendly relationship with Presidents Dacko and Bokassa. His African experience is seen to resemble a black diamond in his heart.

495 **African tales: folklore of the Central African Republic, as told by village
     story-tellers, translated by Polly Strong.**
     Polly Strong. Mogadore, Ohio: Telcraft, 1992. 97p.

African tales are told and retold under the shade of a tree, and around the village fires where the shadows erase the sharpness of the visible world and flame and embers enhance the feeling of magic and suspense. The author, a teacher who lives in Bangui, shares tales (literal Sango-to-English translation) from the oral tradition of the Mandjia and Banda tribes.

496 **La femme-antilope.** (The antelope-woman.)
François Valdi. Paris: André Depeuch, 1928. 188p.

François Ciavaldini, here writes under the pseudonym François Valdi. He was the chief administrator of the colonies, a former journalist, and was head of the subdivision of Bria in 1923. In 1940, Felix Eboué apppointed him Director of Political Affairs and Information for the general government of FEA. The story of the antelope woman is that of the intervention in Banda society of a spirit called *legpa*, which has the head and feet of an antelope and the stomach and shoulders of a man. This *legpa* shows itself in the story when a man condemned to death at the post of Bria is executed. This book deserved the same success as *Batouala* by René Maran, a friend of the author.

Arts and Music

497 **Contes et chantefables ngbaka-mabo (RCA).** (Ngbaka-Mabo tales and
singing fables [CAR].)
Simha Arom. Paris: SELAF, 1970. 238p.
Comments on Ngbaka-Mabo music.

498 **Folk music of the Central African Republic.**
Simha Arom. In: *Grove's Dictionary of Music and Musicians*. London:
Macmillan, 1981. 13p. [6th edition].
Briefly considers the characteristics of current Central African music.

499 **Polyphonies et polyrythmies instrumentales d'Afrique Centrale:
structure et méthodologie.** (The instrumental polyphonies and
polyrhythms of Central Africa: structure and methodology.)
Simha Arom. Paris: SELAF, 1985. 2 vols. (Collection
Ethnomusicologie).
Music has an important place in the life of the central Africans. The author makes a
methodical analysis of the polyphonies of the Aka pygmies, using the method of
playback. This music contains practically no words, only syllables and vowels which
emphasize the voice. The associated myths appear in the form of singing-fables.

500 **L'apprenti fada.** (The apprentice crackpot.)
Yvan Audouard. Paris: Stock, 1979. 176p.
In this collection of anecdotes, the author recounts, under the title of 'the most
beautiful crackpot in the world', his meeting with the central African naïve painter,
Jérôme Ramedane, who died in 1991, in Sibut (p. 117-23).

Arts and Music

501 **Le problème des couteaux de jet africains.** (The problem of African throwing-knives.)
Gérald Berthoud. *Musées de Genève*, no. 61 (January 1964), p. 6-9.
Throwing-knives are used throughout central Africa to determine a cultural area corresponding approximately to populations of the same linguistic group. The knives are made of iron and have multiple heads which, when thrown at prey or an opponent always hit the target with one of the points. They are used in Central Africa in a specific cultural area between the Niger and the Nile, in a zone occupied by peoples belonging to two distinct linguistic family groupings. As such they present intriguing problems to sociologists. The origins of some of these peoples seems to be from marshland where hunting for birds using these strange knives was widespread. In addition, the knives are used for ceremonial purposes in traditional dances and ceremonies.

502 **Les chants à penser des Gbaya en Centrafrique.** (The thinking-songs of the Gbaya in the Central African Republic.)
Vincent Dehoux. Paris: SELAF, 1986. 223p. (Ethnomusicologie Series, no. 2).
The music of the Gbaya consists essentially of repertoires of songs connected, on the one hand, with events which serve as milestones in the life of the group or of the individual, and on the other, with everyday activities. The present study deals with the category of 'thinking songs', a repertory of songs reserved for men and accompanied on the *sanza* (a kind of small traditional guitar which is found throughout the Central African Republic.)

La clef musicale des langages tambourinés et sifflés. (The musical key to drummed and whistled languages.)
See item no. 237.

Statistics

503 **Statistiques monétaires 1981-1990.** (Monetary statistics 1981-90.)
Banque des Etats de l'Afrique Centrale (BEAC: Cameroon, Central
Africa, Congo, Gabon, Equatorial Guinea, Chad). *Monthly Bulletin
of BEAC*, no. 173 (June-July 1990), p. 259-306.

In collaboration with the Office of Statistics of the International Monetary Fund, the
Bank of the States of Central Africa produced these statistics which represent a
revision of monetary statistics previously published in the monthly bulletin *Etudes et
Statistiques*.

504 **Annuaire statistique de la République Centrafricaine.** (Statistical
Yearbook of the Central African Republic.)
Lucien Castelli, Roger Jolivot. Bangui: Ministère de l'Economie
Nationale et de l'Action Rurale, direction de la statistique et de la
conjoncture; Paris: Ministère de la Coopération, 1963. 183p. maps.

This small book contains useful statistical information about the Central African
Republic in the form of tables and graphs. The book is divided into twelve chapters
dealing with: climatology; population, health; education; work; justice; foreign trade;
production; transport; prices; currency and credit; and public finances. The annual
revised editions which were announced have, however, never been completed.

505 **Annuaire des entreprises industrielles et commerciales de la République
Centrafricaine.** (The Yearbook of Industrial and Commercial
Businesses of the Central African Republic.)
Bangui: Chambre de commerce, d'industrie, des mines et de l'artisanat
de la République Centrafricaine, éditions OREC, Douala 1991. 201p.

This catalogue gives a complete list of central African businesses.

506 **Annuaire statistique. Les chiffres sur l'essentiel de l'information économique et sociale.** (Statistical Yearbook: figures on the essential points of economic and social information.)
Bangui: Division des statistiques et des études économiques, Ministère de l'Economie, des Finances, du Plan et de la Coopération Internationale, 1986- . annual.

This annual consists of four chapters: general information about the Central African Republic; production (by sector); national accounts; and living conditions. It is complemented every quarter by the *Quarterly Statistical Bulletin* published in Bangui by the same service, and by a monthly letter also containing statistics. There is also a regional statistical yearbook and an annual study of industrial and commercial businesses.

507 **Annuaire des statistiques.** (The Statistical Yearbook.)
Bangui: Service de statistique du ministère de l'enseignement primaire, secondaire et technique, 1989-90. 169p.

This annual report shows the enormous effort made by the Central African authorities to educate children in a rural environment as well as in the towns. It should be pointed out that the main share of French aid goes to education and that most of the cooperative aid assistants are teachers.

508 **Geographical distribution of financial flows to developing countries.**
Paris: OECD. 1980- . annual.

Tables organized country by country, indicate the amount of foreign aid provided to various developing countries, including the Central African Republic.

509 **The Statesman's Yearbook: Statistical and Historical Annual of the States of the World.**
London: Macmillan, 1864- . annual.

Presents factual information and statistics concerning a wide range of economic, social and political indicators for the states of the world.

510 **UNESCO Statistical Yearbook.**
Paris: UNESCO, 1963- . annual.

Provides statistics concerning education in the various member states.

511 **Statistical Yearbook.**
New York: United Nations, Statistical Office, 1948- . annual.

A wide-ranging compilation of statistics pertaining to each member state of the United Nations.

512 **Demographic Yearbook.**
New York: United Nations, 1948- . annual.

Presents official statistics concerning the populations of the various member states of the United Nations including the Central African Republic.

Bibliographies

513 Bibliographique signalétique sur les missions chrétiennes en Oubangui-Chari, des origines à nos jours. (A descriptive bibliography on the Christian missions in Ubangi-Shari, from their origin to the present day.)
Maurice Amaye. Aix-en-Provence, France: Université d'Aix-en-Provence, IHPOM, 1981. 78p.

This bibliography is useful to all those interested in evangelization in Central Africa. The Catholic and Protestant missionaries are also, of course, very often linguists and ethnographers.

514 Bibliographie centrafricaine. (Central African bibliography.)
Father Ghislain de Banville. Bangui: Maison St. Charles, 1991. 102p.

This bibliography includes 1,750 entries arranged in simple alphabetical order with key words in brackets. The major subject headings are: history; anthropology; linguistics; religion; and politics.

515 Bibliographie de l'AEF. (Bibliography of French Equatorial Africa.)
Georges Bruel. Paris: Larose, 1914. 326p.

This bibliography is almost exhaustive in its coverage of the first twenty years of the colonization of FEA. However, it consists of numerous very small articles of little interest. In a later work (*Bibliographie d'histoire coloniale*, Paris: Société d'histoire des colonies françaises, Roussin et Tramond, 1932. 667p.), Georges Bruel limits his bibliography of FEA to eleven pages.

516 **Bibliographie de la République Centrafricaine relative aux sciences humaines.** (A bibliography of the Central African Republic relating to the humanities.)
Suzanne Jean. Paris: BDPA, 1961. 53p.

The author, an ethnographer, provides a multidisciplinary classification of books and articles that appeared before 1961. Ten pages are devoted to works concerning expeditions and the exploration of the country.

517 **Bibliographie ethnographique de l'AEF (1914-1948).** (An ethnographical bibliography of French Equatorial Africa 1914-48.)
Pierre Sanner. Paris: Imprimerie Nationale, 1949. 107p.

Sanner, a colonial administrator, wrote this work at the request of the Governor-General of the FEA. He presents it as an update of the bibliography (q.v.) compiled by his colleague, Georges Bruel, that appeared in 1914.

518 **Répertoire des mémoires et thèses de licence, maîtrise, DEA et doctorat, soutenues en géographie, histoire, lettres, médecine, sciences.** (A list of dissertations and theses completed for bachelor's and master's degrees and doctorates in the fields of geography, history, arts, medicine and science.)
Université de Bangui, 1982- . annual.

This list contains some interesting theses, many of which have never been published, concerning the Central African Republic.

Biographies

519 Prosper Augouard.

Augustin Berger. *Hommes et Destins, Académie des Sciences d'Outre Mer*, part 2, vol. 1 (1977), p. 29-33.

The activities of Augouard (1852-1921), who was the first Apostolic Vicar of French Upper Congo and Ubangi (1890), were a determining factor in the creation of Congolese and Central African churches. An ardent patriot, he supplied valuable help to the Brazza and Marchand expeditions, in spite of his disputes with an administration that was often anti-colonial. He is criticized, however, for his good relationship with the concessionary companies. (See item no. 266.)

520 Antonin-Marius Vergiat.

Jean Cantournet. *Hommes et Destins, Académie des Sciences d'Outre Mer*, part 9, (1977), p. 473-74.

Vergiat originally went to central Africa to take aerial photographs but he became interested in the customs and religious rites of the Mandjia people. His works, which appeared in 1936 and 1937 were re-edited in 1981. (See items no. 134 and 285.)

521 René Maran.

Marie-Magdeleine Carbet. *Hommes et Destins, Académie des Sciences d'Outre Mer*, part 2, vol. 2 (1977), p. 503-10.

Coming from a colonial family of West Indian origin, René Maran (1887-1960), joined his father in central Africa to serve in the colonial administration. He worked at various posts in Ubangi-Shari, notably in the Banda region. His novel, the story of the life of a Banda chief Batouala ('a novel about negroes, seen from inside, written by a negro') has been enormously successful. On 15 December 1921, it won the Prix Goncourt. This novel was the motivating factor which led André Gide to write *Journey to the Congo*. Expelled from the administration and returning to France in 1925, René Maran devoted himself entirely to literature and the struggle against colonization. (See items no. 480-82.)

522 Georges Toqué.

Robert Cornevin. *Hommes et Destins, Académie des Sciences d'Outre Mer*, part 1 (1975), p. 592-3.

The administrator-historian, Robert Cornevin, recounts the tragic fate of his colleague, Georges Toqué (1879-1920). A young subdivision chief in Upper Shari, he had to fight against the Mandjia uprising. He was used as a scapegoat by the colonial authorities, who were anxious to avoid being denounced for the numerous atrocities committed by the colonists and the state servants in Central Africa. After his removal from office he made his living, with difficulty, as a journalist. He was condemned to death for having given some articles to the *Ardennes Gazette*, a pro-German paper at the time of the occupation, and he was killed by a firing squad on 15 May 1920 at Vincennes. He wrote two books, one on the Banda, the other on the social injustice of the colonial administration in Upper Shari. (See item no. 211.)

523 René Malbrant.

Oswald Durand. *Hommes et Destins, Académie des Sciences d'Outre Mer*, part 1 (1975), p. 422.

This brief biography of René Malbrant (1903-61), by the governor Oswald Durand, celebrates the career of the veterinary surgeon, and head of the Service of Animal Husbandry of the FEA, whose works are still authoritative. Central Africa owes him a great deal for importing his herd of Mbororo cows and the first measures which he took to protect wildlife. As Deputy of the first college for Chad and Ubangui-Shari he engaged in acrimonious political debate with Boganda and became director of a movement for the defence of the colonies in France.

524 Rabah.

Pierre Kalck. *Hommes et Destins, Académie des Sciences d'Outre Mer*, part 1, (1975), p. 495-7. bibliog.

A short biography of Pasha Zubayr's former lieutenant, who after devastating Upper Ubangi, made himself master of Bagirmi and the old empire of Bornu. He was defeated and killed by the French in April 1900. From 1879 to 1890 Rabah stayed in Central Africa.

525 Mohamed ès Senoussi.

Pierre Kalck. *Hommes et Destins, Académie des Sciences d'Outre Mer*, part 1 (1973), p. 568-71. bibliog.

A nephew of Kobur, the Sultan of Dar-al-Kuti, Muhammad as Sanusi was placed on his uncle's throne by Rabah. It was Sanusi's followers who ambushed and killed Paul Crampel, the explorer, on 9 April 1891 (see item no. 529). However, Sanusi managed to pass a protectorate treaty with the French, to avoid any reprisals by his former suzerain, the king of Wadaï. Thus he was able to complete the ruin of Upper Ubangi with impunity, until 1911 when he was killed by a French officer.

Biographies

526 **Felix Eboué, administrateur de brousse.** (Felix Eboué, an administrator in the bush.)
Pierre Kalck.   In: *Actes du Colloque Eboué, Institut des hautes études de défense nationale*, Paris (10 January 1985). Paris: Académie des Sciences d'Outre Mer and Ecole Militaire, 1985, p. 96-101.

Nobody knew better than Felix Eboué, who was subdivision head in Ubangi-Shari for twenty-three years, how to 'reconcile opposites', and prove himself worthy 'of the double administrator's mandate, that of Africa and of France'.

527 **Paul Crampel, (1864-1891) un explorateur du centre de l'Afrique.** (Paul Crampel (1864-91): an explorer in central Africa.)
Pierre Kalck.   Paris: L'Harmattan, 1993. 256p.

Using unpublished documents, this biography emphasizes the eminent place held by this explorer in French colonial history. Crampel became Brazza's secretary in 1887, and in 1888 he explored the north of Gabon, where he was seriously injured. In the following year he headed back to Bangui, at that time the last French base in Ubangi. As the commissioner-general's delegate, he restored security in the region, before making his way towards the north, into unknown territory. His ambition was to reach Chad, then Algeria. He was assassinated on 9 April 1891 not far from the River Aouk, the present-day southern border of the Republic of Chad. His great plan was adopted by the Committee of French Africa and was finally realized in 1900. Crampel can be considered as being the founder of French Ubangi, which became the Central African Republic.

528 **Emile Gentil.**
Bernard Lanne.   *Hommes et Destins, Académie des Sciences d'Outre Mer*, part 4 (1981), p. 331-37. bibliog.

Emile Gentil (1866-1914), a ship's ensign then colonial administrator, accompanied Brazza in Upper Sangha, before being appointed commander of the circle of Mobaye. In 1896 Emile Gentil was placed in charge of an expedition which aimed to reach Lake Chad. He took possession of the Banda, Mandja and Sara lands between Ubangi and Shari. In addition, he made various treaties of alliance and protection with Sanusi, the Sultan of Dar-al-Kuti and Gaourang, the leader of the Bagirmi. Gentil reached the shores of Lake Chad on 1 November 1897. As a result of the treaties made with the two leaders, and because of the weapons that were sent from France to support them, Rabah launched an offensive on Gentil and his expedition in the Shari region. On 22 April 1900 Gentil overthrew Rabah's army at Kousseri thanks to reinforcements that came from two other French expeditions coming from Algeria and Senegal. Emile Gentil was considered to be the man who brought the Crampel plan of 1891 to fruition. He was appointed governor of the colonies in 1900 at the age of 34, and in 1904 became Commissioner General of the government in the French Congo at a time when the colony was in deep crisis. He had to face serious incidents which had occurred as the result of abuses committed by the concessionary companies and the bureaucrats (in particular the problems in Bangui and Upper Shari). He was recalled to France, in poor health, and in 1908 he was appointed a tax collector in Gironde.

529 **Felix Eboué, grand commis et loyal serviteur (1885-1994).** (Felix Eboué, a top-ranking and loyal servant, 1885-1944.)
René Maran. Paris: Editions Penone, 1957. 128p.
The author of *Batouala* lets the friendship and admiration he held for Felix Eboué shine through this biography. The administrator Eboué had earlier been persecuted by the authorities for his links with the writer René Maran.

530 **Felix-Adolphe-Sylvestre Eboué.**
Albert Maurice. *Hommes et Destins, Académie des Sciences d'Outre Mer*, part 1 (1975), p. 212-15.
The son of a Guianan gold-digger, Felix Eboué (1884-1944), qualified at the Ecole Coloniale, and served in Upper Ubangi from 1909. He stayed there until 1932, when he was appointed secretary-general in Martinique. He became governor of Chad in 1939, and declared the union of this territory with Free France on 26 August 1940. General de Gaulle named him Governor-General of French Equatorial Africa. It was he who instigated and organized the Brazzaville African Conference in 1944. Eboué (q.v.) was alo an ethnographer and linguist.

531 **Barthélemy Boganda, Antoine Darlan, Jane Vialle. Trois représentants oubangiens du 2ème collège. 1946-1952.** (Barthèlemy Boganda, Antoine Darlan, Jane Vialle. Three Ubangian representatives of the 2nd college, 1946-52.)
Jean-Dominique Penel. Bangui: Université de Bangui, 1985. 205p.
The author recounts the activities of the first three elected members of Ubangi-Shari (2nd college). Boganda was a Deputy in the French National Assembly, Darlan was an advisor to the Assembly of the French Union and Vialle was a Senator.

532 **L'itinéraire de Felix Eboué, grand commis de l'Etat jusqu'en 1940.** (The itinerary of Felix Eboué, senior civil servant until 1940.)
Louis Sanmarco. *Actes du Colloque Eboué. Institut des hautes études de défense nationale et Académie des Sciences d'Outre Mer, Ecole Militaire, Paris* (10 January 1985), p. 81-95.
As this account shows, General de Gaulle appointed Eboué as Governor-General of the FEA to show that France was not racist; Eboué was a black originally from Guyana.

533 **Auguste Lamblin.**
Jacques Serre. *Hommes et Destins, Académie des Sciences d'Outre Mer*, part 8, *Gouverneurs, Administrateurs, Magistrats* (1988), p. 229-32.
Auguste Lamblin (1870-1946) directed the colony of Ubangi-Shari for more than ten years (1919-29). He worked harder by far than any other governor to develop the territory. He was responsible for saving the country and also the people who were drained by forced labour as porters and as wild-rubber gatherers.

Biographies

534 Louis Mizon.

Jacques Serre. *Hommes et Destins, Académie des Sciences d'Outre Mer*, part 8, *Gouverneurs, Administrateurs, Magistrats*, (1988), p. 290-95.

Mizon, the lieutenant of the vessel *Mizon*, who discovered that his expedition conflicted with the terms of the Anglo-French Convention of 1890, was able in 1892 to cross Adamawa to Sangha accompanied by a lightly-armed contingent of men without firing a shot.

535 Marie-François-Joseph Clozel.

Jacques Serre. *Hommes et Destins, Académie des Sciences d'Outre Mer*, part 8, *Gourverneurs, Administrateurs, Magistrats*, (1988), p. 84-9.

Clozel was the explorer in charge of the last expedition of the French African Committee, and left Sangha for Chad. At Brazzaville, he learned of the Franco-German Convention (1893) which granted Germany access to Chad through Cameroon. He therefore limited himself to the exploration of Upper Sangha. (See item no. 110.)

536 Gilbert-Georges Bruel.

Marcel Soret. *Hommes et Destins, Académie des Sciences d'Outre Mer*, part 4 (1981), p. 135-45.

Bruel was colonial administrator in Upper Shari at the beginning of the century, and loved geography and ethnography. He was the author of the only comprehensive works on the FEA until the 1930s. His numerous personal archives, left at the Academy for Science Overseas, have been classified and an inventory has been made of them by Jean Cantournet. (See item no. 1.)

537 Memorial du Souvenir Français-Bangui 1889-1989. (Chronicles of French memorials: Bangui 1889-1989.)

Jean-Marie Thiébaut. Bangui: Le Souvenir français (1990). 134p.

During a long and patient project to update our knowledge of historical tombs and French monuments located in Central Africa, the author found and identified multiple tombs abandoned to the bush or to oblivion. In the notes, classified by locality, he allows us to discover the lives of these dead people. This martyrology represents a valuable collection of biographies relating to the history of the country.

538 Eboué.

Brian Weinstein. New York: Oxford University Press (1972). 350p.

This book is currently the best biography available of the Governor-General, Felix Eboué. The author wrote this work after carrying out minutely detailed research in the places where Eboué lived, particularly in Central Africa.

Historical Dictionary of the Central African Republic.

See item no. 180.

Barthélemy Boganda, tribun et visionnaire de l'Afrique Centrale. (Barthélemy Boganda, Central Africa's tribune and visionary.)
See item no. 179.

Karnou, prophète de l'indépendance en Afrique Centrale. (Karnou, prophet of independence in Central Africa.)
See item no. 189.

Indexes

There follow three separate indexes: authors (personal and corporate); titles; and subjects. Title entries are italicized and refer either to the main titles, or to other works cited in the annotations. The numbers refer to bibliographic entry rather than page numbers. Individual index entries are arranged in alphabetical sequence.

Index of Authors

133

Index of Titles

Index of Subjects

A

Abandia *see* Bandia (dynasties)
Académie des Sciences 97
Académie des Sciences d'outre-mer 178, 181 *see also* Biographies
Académie des Sciences morales et politiques 393
Académie Française 471, 479
Adamawa 534
Administration and technical services 3, 8
Agoudou-Manga (locality) 435
Agreements 360
Agriculture, forestry and animal husbandry 50, 407
Agriculture agricultural agroclimatology 28, 432
agricultural calendars 113
agricultural conditions 305
agricultural development 433
agricultural situation 429
agricultural survey 293
Boukoko research station 105, 426
Bureau pour le développement de la production agricole 410, 444
land clearing 447
coffee 383, 407, 423, 425, 427, 431, 438
cola tree 426
cotton 317, 380, 383, 385, 394, 417, 428, 443, 463
by-products 491

Dario (village) 309
Institut de recherches sur le coton et les textiles tropicaux 417, 430, 442
Institut français pour le café et le cacao 92, 423, 426-427, 431
Institut national agronomique 428-429, 433, 447
mechanized agricultural methods 436
Pouyamba (village) 306
Roselle 430
rural development 418
villages 122
soils 19-20, 28, 33, 43, 46, 91, 432
traditional 422, 445
Aiki *see* Rounga (Runga) and Peoples
Aka *see* Peoples (Pygmies)
Algeria 74, 471, 527
Algiers 167
Americans 149
Animal husbandry
animals for draught 435
bee-keeping 424, 439
cattle breeding 412, 422, 435, 440, 445
Fulbé, Mbororo 413
Institut d'Élevage et de Médecine Vétérinaire Tropicale 411-412, 414, 416, 419, 421-422, 424, 445-446
livestock development 411, 415
meat 411, 414
monitors manual 440
pastoral development in the West 413
ranching 416
Tsé-Tsé fly 419, 422
Trypanoresistant cattle 445

Trypanotolerant cattle 422
veterinary surgeon (Desrotour, Jean) 421
Aouk (river) 527
Anzica, Anziques 200 *see also* Kingdom of the Congo, history
Archeology 217
Architects 332
Archives 373
Arts and music 457-502
Augouard, Mgr. Prosper (apostolic vicar) 299, 519 *see also* Missionary activity
Azandé *see* Zandé, peoples, languages

B

Bagirmi, Baguirmi (kingdom) 65-66, 149, 524 *see also* History
Bahr al-Ghazal, Bahr el-Ghazal 79, 128-129, 133, 142, 169, 188, 259
Baja *see* Ngbaya
Bakouma (locality) 42
Bambari (locality) 136, 237, 303, 357
Bana 324 *see also* Initiate societies
Banda 52, 68, 70, 82, 85, 101, 110, 112, 121, 128, 136, 220, 229, 231-232, 236-237, 246, 263, 285, 305, 308, 312-313, 316, 321, 326, 420, 435-436, 480, 482, 495-496, 521, *see also* Peoples, History, Languages
Bandia (dynasties) 57, 66, 140, 152, 190, 294, 492 *see also* Abandia
Bandimbakolo 475 *see also* Folklore

Bangui 9, 29, 73, 87, 127, 142, 147, 160, 167, 206, 213, 233, 267, 281, 325, 334, 338-339, 341-343, 345-346, 405, 408, 455, 464-465, 472, 495 *see also* Urbanization
agriculture 339, 343, 345
diet and supplies in Bangui 338
evolution 326-327, 330
fire-wood 329
foundation 144
historical and geographical study 344
landed property 340
local administration 337
map-guide of Bangui 37
master-plan 332
origins 168, 186, 193
points of view and witness reports 143
prostitution 333
rural environment 336
shanty-towns 335
site 324
Bangui-Chad railway 404-405 *see also* Economy, Transport
Bangui magnetic anomaly 27, 35
Banks
Bank of States of Central Africa 503
World Bank 415
Bantu 230
Banziri, Gbanziri 190, 227, 326, *see also* Peoples, Languages
Baoulé 422, *see also* Animal husbandry (cattle)
Baram-Bakié *see also* History (chief)
Batouala 481-483, 496, 521, 529 *see also* Literature
Baya (east) *see* Kreich, Kresch
Baya (west) *see* Gbaya
Baya war *see* Kongo Wara war, History

Berberati 65, 119, 278
Berlin, conference on African affairs 207 *see also* History
Bétaré-Oya (Cameroon) 116
Bibliographies 513-518
Biographies 519-538
Biscarrat 83, *see also* Crampel expedition
Bureau International du Travail 72
Boda (locality) 117, 493
Bodoé (tribe) 249
Boffi (tribe) 117
Boganda, Barthélemy (priest, deputy, president) 170, 179, 270, 351, 354, 358, 377, 493, 523, 531, *see also* History, Biographies
Bokassa, Jean-Bedel (colonel, general, marshal, president, emperor) 135, 156, 163, 166, 196, 199, 216, 281, 347-348, 358, 364-365, 375, 384, 400, 460, 463, 466, 469, 494 *see also* History, Biographies
Bomu *see* Mbomou, Mbomu
Bondjo 127 *see also* Peoples
Bondo (Zaïre) 109
Bonnel de Mézières expedition 66
Borders 18, 74, 84, 207
Bordier, Paul (governor) 352
Bornu, empire of 524 *see also* History
Bororo *see* Fulbé
Bougbou 190, 212 *see also* Peoples
Boukoko 105, 126 *see also* Agriculture
Boundaries *see* Borders
Bozum (locality) 119, 130, 357

Brazza (commision of inquiry) 145, 204 *see also* History
Brazzaville 170, 189, 211
Brazzaville conference 330, 357
Bria (locality) 196
Briand, Doctor Joseph 160
Bruel, Georges 178, 517, 536
Buffalo 99 *see also* Hunting
Burundi 355
Bush fires 97, 104
Bwaka 123 *see also* Peoples

C

Cameroon 116, 150, 281, 355, 413-414
Canada 460
Canadian Association of African Studies 255
Cannibalism 66, 299
Capucin missionaries 278, *see also* Missionary activity
Caravans routes 18
Carnot (locality) 30, 60
Cartography *see* Geography, Geology, Maps
Census of the population 293, 326, 330 *see also* Population
Centre des hautes études sur l'Afrique et l'Asie modernes 319, 351-352, 355, 400
Centre National de la Recherche Scientifique 132, 246, 312
Chad 53, 74, 78, 162, 164, 167, 177, 194, 248, 314, 355, 428, 484, 523, 527, 535
Chari *see* Shari
Chevalier expedition, Chevalier, Professor Auguste 67, 97, 104
Children 316, 455
Chronology 180

Map of the Central African Republic

This map shows the more important towns and other features.

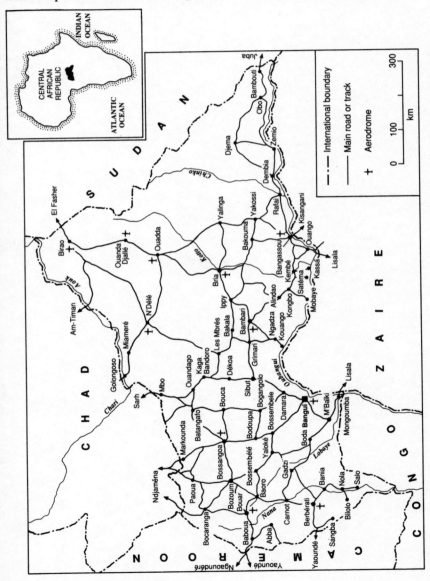